A TALE OF TWO GRANDFATHERS

A Tale of Two Grandfathers

OWEN LLOYD GEORGE

BELLEW • LONDON

1999

First published in Great Britain in 1999 by
Bellew Publishing Company Limited
8 Balham Hill, London SW12 9EA

ISBN 1 85725 150 4

Typeset by Antony Gray
Printed and bound in Great Britain by
MPG Books Ltd, Bodmin, Cornwall

*To Jo who knows
all the stories*

Preface

THE IDEA for this book arose out of a suggestion by one of my children that I should set down what I remembered of my two grandfathers, David Lloyd George and Robert McAlpine, and this undertaking gradually developed to encompass my own life-story. One's memory of events fifty or sixty years ago can often be faulty and if I have stumbled in portraying distant family episodes the error is solely mine.

In describing my McAlpine grandfather's early days I owe a debt of gratitude to the biography of him written in 1925 by an American, J. Saxon Childers, who had the benefit of a number of conversations with him in old age.

I have also quoted freely from the published diaries of the late-lamented A. J. Sylvester, who was LG's principal private secretary for the last twenty-five years of his life, and who was a close and well-loved friend of the family.

Many old friends have given me help and advice in composing this book, none more than Kenneth Rose, who not only corrected my grammar in places but who jogged my memory over certain incidents in which we shared a wartime experience.

Above all, I am immensely grateful to Ruth Johnson, who has valiantly typed my ill-written manuscript over several years, and who, together with her husband Tom, encouraged me to persevere to the point of finding a publisher.

Owen Lloyd George

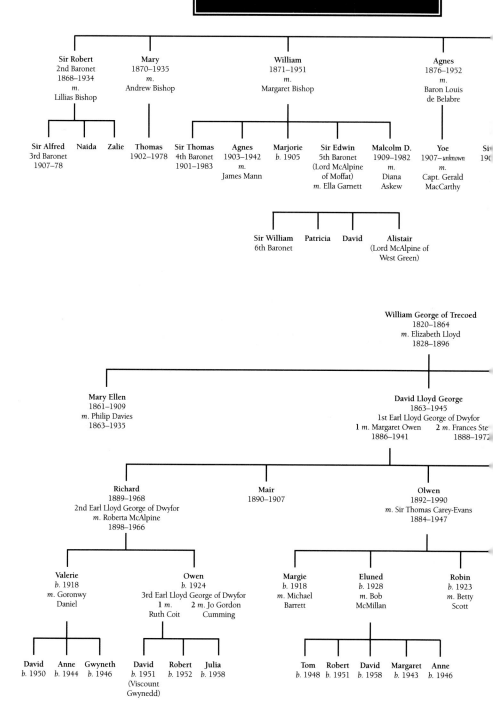

THE McALPINE FAMILY TREE

Sir Robert
2nd Baronet
1868–1934
m.
Lillias Bishop

Mary
1870–1935
m.
Andrew Bishop

William
1871–1951
m.
Margaret Bishop

Agnes
1876–1952
m.
Baron Louis
de Belabre

Sir Alfred
3rd Baronet
1907–78

Naida

Zalie

Thomas
1902–1978

Sir Thomas
4th Baronet
1901–1983

Agnes
1903–1942
m.
James Mann

Marjorie
b. 1905

Sir Edwin
5th Baronet
(Lord McAlpine
of Moffat)
m. Ella Garnett

Malcolm D.
1909–1982
m.
Diana
Askew

Yoe
1907–*unknown*
m.
Capt. Gerald
MacCarthy

Si*
190

Sir William
6th Baronet

Patricia

David

Alistair
(Lord McAlpine of
West Green)

William George of Trecoed
1820–1864
m. Elizabeth Lloyd
1828–1896

Mary Ellen
1861–1909
m. Philip Davies
1863–1935

David Lloyd George
1863–1945
1st Earl Lloyd George of Dwyfor
1 *m.* Margaret Owen   2 *m.* Frances Ste*
1886–1941   1888–197*

Richard
1889–1968
2nd Earl Lloyd George of Dwyfor
m. Roberta McAlpine
1898–1966

Mair
1890–1907

Olwen
1892–1990
m. Sir Thomas Carey-Evans
1884–1947

Valerie
b. 1918
m. Goronwy
Daniel

Owen
b. 1924
3rd Earl Lloyd George of Dwyfor
1 *m.*   2 *m.* Jo Gordon
Ruth Coit   Cumming

Margie
b. 1918
m. Michael
Barrett

Eluned
b. 1928
m. Bob
McMillan

Robin
b. 1923
m. Betty
Scott

David
b. 1950

Anne
b. 1944

Gwyneth
b. 1946

David
b. 1951
(Viscount
Gwynedd)

Robert
b. 1952

Julia
b. 1958

Tom
b. 1948

Robert
b. 1951

David
b. 1958

Margaret
b. 1943

Anne
b. 1946

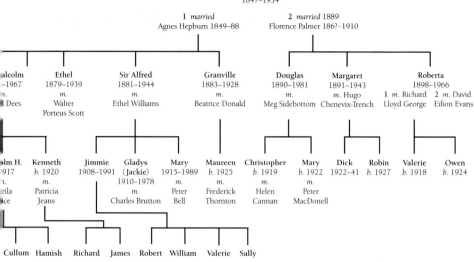

Sir Robert McAlpine 1st Baronet
1847–1934

1 *married*
Agnes Hepburn 1849–88

2 *married* 1889
Florence Palmer 186?–1910

| alcolm –1967 n. l Dees | Ethel 1879–1939 *m.* Walter Porteus Scott | Sir Alfred 1881–1944 *m.* Ethel Williams | Granville 1883–1928 *m.* Beatrice Donald | Douglas 1890–1981 *m.* Meg Sidebottom | Margaret 1891–1943 *m.* Hugo Chenevix-Trench | Roberta 1898–1966 1 *m.* Richard Lloyd George 2 *m.* David Eifion Evans |

| lm H. 917 n. eila ice | Kenneth b. 1920 *m.* Patricia Jeans | Jimmie 1908–1991 | Gladys (Jackie) 1910–1978 *m.* Charles Brutton | Mary 1915–1989 *m.* Peter Bell | Maureen b. 1925 *m.* Frederick Thornton | Christopher b. 1919 *m.* Helen Cannan | Mary b. 1922 *m.* Peter MacDonell | Dick 1922–41 | Robin b. 1927 | Valerie b. 1918 | Owen b. 1924 |

Cullum Hamish Richard James Robert William Valerie Sally

THE LLOYD GEORGE FAMILY TREE

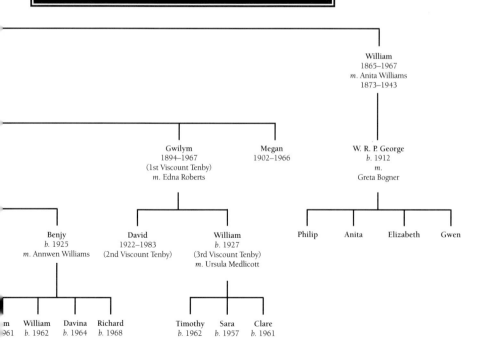

William
1865–1967
m. Anita Williams
1873–1943

| Gwilym 1894–1967 (1st Viscount Tenby) *m.* Edna Roberts | Megan 1902–1966 | W. R. P. George b. 1912 *m.* Greta Bogner |

Benjy
b. 1925
m. Annwen Williams

David
1922–1983
(2nd Viscount Tenby)

William
b. 1927
(3rd Viscount Tenby)
m. Ursula Medlicott

Philip Anita Elizabeth Gwen

m 961 William b. 1962 Davina b. 1964 Richard b. 1968

Timothy b. 1962 Sara b. 1957 Clare b. 1961

Contents

A TALE OF TWO GRANDFATHERS

The author

CHAPTER I

Beginnings

I was conceived in a first-class cabin of the Cunarder *Majestic* while the liner was returning from New York. I would not risk making such an unusual assertion were it not for the fact that not one but both of my parents confirmed the fact to me many years later.

As a result I arrived in the world on 28 April 1924 in my father's house near Chelmsford, in a small hamlet called Springfield.

I returned to that part of Essex some years ago but not a trace of my birthplace remained: it was well and truly buried beneath the A12. But in the twenties it was a peaceful rural area, the only noise being from the steam train that thundered at regular intervals behind the greenhouses and which I found singularly soothing as a child.

The Cottage, as it was called, had undergone so many additions that it was hard to know its original period. At the time of my arrival it must have been predominantly Victorian, with a conservatory, which doubled as the front door, and a balcony above that led out of my parents' bedroom. The drawing-room was originally two rooms and on a different level from the dining-room, and the morning-room had clearly been tacked on later.

There was a pleasant but rather dull garden and there were a few fields in which my father was already indulging his passion for farming (on a small scale), with cows and chickens and his old charger from army days, which was ignominiously harnessed to a mower at hay-making time.

My sister Valerie was six when I was born; not only did she arrive on St Valentine's Day 1918, but my father was at that moment at St Valéry, at the front, so her name was an obvious choice. In spite of the gap in our ages she played with me when I became mobile and was reasonably tolerant of my presence. However, I quickly grew a most remarkable head of golden curls which drew admiring remarks from relations and visitors, which must have been irritating to her, and we had our ups and downs. But I am happy to state that for many years now we have had a close and affectionate relationship that has survived many vicissitudes.

My father, Richard Lloyd George,* was thirty-five when I was born. The eldest of the five Lloyd George children, he found being his father's son a mixed blessing. Although his early childhood was happy enough, born as he was at Mynydd Ednyfed, Criccieth – my great-grandfather Richard Owen's farm – and having early lessons from the redoubtable Richard Lloyd, he was packed off to Dulwich College at the age of eleven. This coincided with the Boer War, of which LG was an outspoken and fiery opponent; indeed his pro-Boer sympathies were nearly to cost him his life.

In consequence of this my father was badly treated and even bullied at Dulwich, until my grandmother discerned what was happening and took him away. At the Portmadoc County School he thrived, and went on to Christ's College, Cambridge in 1908, where he took the tripos exams in scientific engineering with honours.

Being the eldest and being particularly close to his mother, it was not difficult for him to sense the tensions that arose between his parents as a result of LG's philandering. He confronted his father over his behaviour on more than one occasion, which did not make for a sound father-son relationship, and, although he may have had his own failings in later life, I believe that he was damaged psychologically during those tender formative years. He had a first-class brain, an amazing memory, enormous charm, gentleness and a keen sense of humour.

After Cambridge, he became an Associate Member of the Institution of Civil Engineers and spent some time in Spain, learning the language as a preliminary to going to work for S. Pearson & Sons in Central and South America to build railways. At that time Pearson's was among the largest civil engineering contractors in the world; after South America my father found himself helping in the construction of the first Hudson

* Always called Dick

The author and Valerie at The Cottage

The author, Roberta, Uncle Jack (Owain Evans), Dick, Nurse Dyer and Valerie at The Cottage

tunnel in New York and was still abroad in 1914 when war broke out. He returned to England at once to enlist.

He was commissioned first into the Welch Regiment but, because of his engineering background, was asked to transfer to the Royal Engineers. He served in France for almost the entire campaign, being buried alive on two occasions and enduring the horrors of Mametz in July 1916, with the 38th (Welsh) Division. In Robert Graves's words:

> Today I found in Mametz Wood
> A certain cure for lust of blood. . .

The First World War left him, as it left so many others, scarred in mind if not in body. He had married my mother during the war and after demobilisation in 1919 he took up a post with a Glasgow firm of engineers called, I believe, McFarlane's. This was not a full-time occupation so, as my mother had money of her own, they were able to enjoy themselves and travel extensively.

My mother was the youngest child of Sir Robert McAlpine, first baronet and founder of the family firm He was born in 1847, in the humblest of homes at Newarthill, in Lanarkshire, and his life story has always enthralled me almost as much as that of my other grandfather.

His father died when he was five and a half and at the age of seven he got his first job carrying miners' picks to the blacksmith to be sharpened. At eight he was allowed to go down into the local pits where he became a 'trapper', opening and shutting the door as a loaded car of coal went from the face to the mouth of the pit. He was then promoted to a 'drawer', pushing the wagons, and after three years he was earning the princely sum of eight shillings and fourpence a month (about fifteen pounds in 1994).

At the age of eighteen he left the mines and became a bricklayer, thus starting on the road to becoming a building contractor. His first big chance, which offered a possible fifty pounds profit, was a project which had to be completed in a week and required a lot of men, whom he did not have the money to pay. He pawned his watch, borrowed eleven pounds from the butcher and got the job.

Over six feet tall and sturdily built, he had immense stamina and could comfortably lay two thousand bricks a day. By the time he was twenty-eight he owned two brickyards, employed a thousand men and was making an annual profit of seven thousand pounds. The coalfields around Hamilton were expanding rapidly, new housing was urgently needed – and Grandad built the houses.

He had married Agnes Hepburn, whose father was an elder in the local church, when he was in his early twenties, and by the time he was thirty, they had five children. It was in 1877 that disaster struck. Grandad had put all his hard-earned wealth (thirty thousand pounds, about a million pounds today) in the City of Glasgow Bank, which failed that year. Many others were struck down at the same time and debtors and creditors were soon chasing each other in circles. It was a matter of starting again from the beginning. At length, he secured a contract but needed two thousand pounds to pay the men and buy materials. The local manager of the North of Scotland Bank took a tough line: 'But, Mr McAlpine, you have no security.'

'I'll come back tomorrow.'

The following day the discussions followed much the same pattern: 'You still haven't shown me any security, Mr McAlpine.'

'One moment,' Grandad said and went to the door. 'Come in, boys,' he called and his two eldest sons filed in. 'There's my security,' he announced.

He got his loan, and it was the start of an association with the Clydesdale Bank (as it subsequently became) that has lasted to this day.

Before the early reverse, when he had a comfortable home and a loving wife and children about him, he contemplated semi-retirement to indulge in his passion for astronomy, for which he ordered an enormous telescope. After the crash, once he had re-established himself he never stopped working again. It took years to clear all the debts. One day, forty years later, he was being driven through Glasgow when he called to his chauffeur to stop. He hailed an elderly man who was hobbling along the pavement, beckoned him to the car and said, 'You may not know me but I know you; you are my old carting contractor and I owe you some money.' Thirty pounds with five per cent interest was pressed into the astonished but delighted ancient's hand.

It was during the 1880s that Grandad established himself as a successful building contractor. In 1883, the firm was awarded the nine-hundred-thousand-pound contract for the new Singer Manufacturing Company, at Kilbowie, near Glasgow. Several important railways followed: the Lanarkshire and Ayrshire Railway in 1885, part of the Glasgow Subway and, most exciting of all, the West Highland Railway, which nearly cost him his life. This line had to cross the remote Rannoch Moor, and in February 1892, Grandad and six other men set out to survey the route. After three days of worsening weather they were only partly across the wild and treacherous bog; one by one the party succumbed to exhaustion and cold; only Grandad had the strength left to push on, until, when he was all but done, he stumbled upon a shepherd's hut and summoned help.

Years later, as a schoolboy, I travelled on the footplate of a locomotive from Fort William to Mallaig and saw some of the challenges that the building of this railway had presented. One tunnel did a complete figure S in its length – the result of its having to circumvent gushing springs in the heart of the mountain. I marvelled too at the magnificent Glenfinnan Viaduct, an elegant curving structure of twenty-one arches, built of mass concrete; almost Grandad's trademark, the material earned him the

Sir Robert McAlpine, 1st Baronet

Glenfinnan Viaduct, West Highland Railway

sobriquet 'Concrete Bob'. The monument to Bonnie Prince Charlie lies just below the viaduct, close to where he raised his standard in 1745.

Grandad's first wife, and mother of his eight eldest children, died in 1888. In 1889 he was building the Strabane and Letterkenny Railway in Ireland when he met and married Florence Palmer, the daughter of a doctor from County Armagh. From this marriage came three more children, Douglas (b.1890), Margaret (b.1891) and Roberta, my mother (b.1898). There was therefore a difference of thirty years between her and her eldest half-brother, Robert.

My Irish grandmother was known as a woman of 'beauty and wit' who took a keen interest in the supernatural, possessing 'second sight' which occasionally enabled her to have a vision of a friend at the precise time of his or her death. Recently I was asked to contribute to a collection of tales of the supernatural and wrote the following:

Margaret, Douglas and Roberta with their mother

My maternal grandmother was Irish and the daughter of a Dublin doctor. Sometime in the 1880s, when she was about seventeen years old, she was going to stay in the country with a schoolfriend. She left the train at the small country town only to find she had made a mistake as to the time of her arrival and was half an hour early. As it was a fine June afternoon, she decided to go for a stroll and walked out of the town to a small loch, where she sat down to enjoy the scenery.

Quite suddenly, she felt distinctly chilled and uncomfortable – and the sun appeared to go in. At that moment, from over her right shoulder, she was aware of a tall man approaching, dressed in a long, heavy tweed coat; the figure walked straight past her into the loch and disappeared beneath the water.

The blackness that had descended over her lifted, the sun shone again and she returned to the railway station where her friend and her father were waiting in a pony and trap.

On the journey home, she recounted what had happened, and

when they reached her friend's house, her father asked my grand-mother again exactly what had happened by the loch. Being a professional man and very meticulous, he took the trouble to write down the precise details.

A week later, the local butcher committed suicide at exactly the spot where my grandmother had been sitting; he had filled the pockets of his heavy tweed overcoat with weights from his shop scales and walked into the loch.*

Sadly I never knew this unusual forebear as she died when my mother was only twelve.

My mother adored her father and he was always her 'beau ideal', against whom all other men had to be measured. To her, determina-tion – the will to see a thing through to the end – was a vital component in anyone's character. This and straight dealing in every-thing were uppermost in her attitude to life. As a young girl she was full of life and fun; the late Ian Stewart – a close friend of the present McAlpine family whose father was stationmaster at Dalmuir, near to where the family lived – gave me a graphic account of my mother doing a spirited solo dance aged ten or so. She grew to love dancing and was very good at it, especially exotic South American numbers, including, of course, the tango.

After her mother's death she spent much of her childhood at Marchwiel, in North Wales, where her half-brother Alfred and his wife had settled. Alfred, who was Grandad's fourth son, was in charge of the Midlands and Welsh side of McAlpine's. This was my mother's first introduction to Wales.

It is not absolutely clear to me how my parents came to meet, but it certainly happened at Bath, in 1917. I believe Grandad must have gone there to take the waters – he was seventy at the time – and stayed at the Empire Hotel with his two youngest daughters, Margaret and Roberta, who was then eighteen. My father was in the local Red Cross hospital, recuperating from trench fever, and somehow he and Roberta met, fell

* Ben Noakes, *I Saw a Ghost*, Weidenfeld & Nicolson, 1986

in love and agreed to marry, all very quickly. Photographs of my mother at this time show her still with a schoolgirlish look (she had just left Cheltenham Ladies' College), but with those wonderful blue eyes, clear complexion and abundant brown hair that were my childish recollections of her and were features of the beauty which stayed with her all her life.

They were married on 7 April in Bath Abbey, which entailed a long walk up that majestic aisle, with a large congregation on either side. Then back across the green to the Empire Hotel for a reception which, alas, had to be teetotal. Lloyd George, who had become Prime Minister four months before, had in 1915 persuaded the King to forswear drink in the royal household for the duration of the war as an example to the country and to try to reduce drunkenness, which LG said was causing more loss of production than German submarines. Though it was an unpopular measure (Kenneth Rose in his *George V* describes how 'a crape wreath was fastened to the cellar door and Charlie Cust fainted the first night after dinner'), the King stoically stuck to his self-denial and naturally expected his First Minister to do the same. However, there was apparently a small room at the reception to which various McAlpine uncles retreated at intervals, returning with heightened colour and raised spirits.

After a short honeymoon my father returned to his regiment in France and my mother moved to Wales.

CHAPTER 2

Taid and Nain[*]

My parents' first home, which they rented, was Plas Hen (today Plas Talhenbont) at Llanystumdwy, close to the River Dwyfach and only a mile and a half from my grandparents' home at Criccieth. It was here that my sister Valerie was born on 14 February 1918, the first grand-child of David and Margaret Lloyd George, my much loved grandparents.

My grandmother (whom we always called 'Nain', as we called our grandfather 'Taid') was the only child of Richard and Mary Owen. I cannot do better than quote from my father's book[†] on his mother which he wrote as a loving filial tribute after her death.

> She was born on 4 November 1886, at Mynydd Edynyfed Fawr (the family farm), to which my grandparents had moved from Dolwgan, high upon the hill above Criccieth. Through her father she could trace her descent from Owen Gwynedd, a twelfth-century Prince of Gwynedd, or North Wales. On her mother's side she was a descend-ant of Hywel Dda (Howell the Good), a tenth-century Prince of Wales famed as the Welsh Law-Giver. Thus, like her parents, she was *boneddiges*, the embodiment of the best in Welsh culture as it flourishes in farming families, with their code, their tradition and their roots deep in the past of the countryside.

> Her courtship by David Lloyd George has been well documented by

---

[*] pronounced 'tide' and 'nine'
[†] *Dame Margaret*, George Allen & Unwin, 1947

above Dick on leave at Plas Talhenbont, 1917
below Roberta at Plas Talhenbont

several talented writers, so I will only say that it is a tribute to my grandfather's tenacity that the day was finally won, for he was not only a Baptist, while the Owens were staunch Calvinistic Methodists, but – even worse – a Liberal with strong Radical tendencies. But married they duly were, in 1888, and my father was born at Mynydd Ednyfed (now the club house of Criccieth Golf Club) the following February, a year before Lloyd George entered Parliament.

Four more children followed. Mair (1890), who died tragically at the early age of seventeen, Olwen (1892), Gwilym (1894) and Megan (1902). I shall refer frequently to these my aunts and uncle, as I saw them from a child's viewpoint, in later pages, but for the moment I will keep my grandmother in focus.

I have already mentioned the difficulties my father encountered as a boy and a young man, intervening between his parents. It was my grandmother though who had to cope on a daily basis with this mercurial husband for whom frequent affairs with women of all sorts, married and unmarried, was a form of compulsion. And yet the only person whom he deeply loved all his life was 'old Maggie', his bedrock. She has been criticised for leaving him alone in London during their early married life, but she genuinely felt that she could give her rapidly growing family a better start in life in Criccieth. Later on, when he had gained office and could spend less and less time in his constituency of Caernarvon Boroughs, it was she who fought his elections for him, kept the local Liberal Association happy, and above all quieted the suspicious mutterings from the chapel folk who had voted for him.

She was no fool and he was not always particularly adroit at covering his tracks so many a confrontation ensued, but she always forgave him in the end. She had a matchless serenity, coupled with an impish sense of humour that we all came to know and love.

I have already spoken of my father's unhappiness at school at the time of the Boer War; her swift appreciation of the situation and firm action to deal with it were typical. She could not abide any form of injustice. Later that same year LG spoke against the war in Birmingham, in the heart of Joseph Chamberlain's own country, and was nearly lynched; my grandmother had to wait many hours before she knew that he had survived – smuggled out of the City Hall disguised as a policeman. They were both independent spirits; each had been to some extent spoilt in their early years, she as an only child of doting parents and he as the favourite of his uncle Richard Lloyd who brought him up.

I think this quality of independence made a great contribution to their mutual attraction. Nain (as I shall henceforth refer to her) admired her husband immensely but was never in awe of him, and would not hesitate to tell him what she thought. He, for his part, respected her opinions, left the upbringing of the children entirely to her, and when, in 1900, they had their first genuine family home in London, near Wandsworth Common, he happily concurred when she insisted on having every servant recruited from Criccieth, so that, in my father's phrase, 'once you were across the threshhold, you were in Wales'.

The dominant figure in this establishment was Sarah Jones, or 'Lallie' as she was forever known in the family. Although she came originally as nurse to Megan, her duties expanded to all departments, including helping my grandfather to dress. He was always quite hopeless with his fingers and incapable even of tying his shoelaces. (In that otherwise admirable television series *The Life and Times of David Lloyd George*, there was a sequence showing him as a young man riding a bicycle; if he had ever got on a bicycle he would have fallen off within yards.) Lallie remained with the family for over fifty years and was always the first person we grandchildren sought out on arrival at Criccieth.

This strong Welsh family atmosphere in my grandparents' various homes was by no means lessened when they later moved first to No. 11 and then to No. 10 Downing Street. From 1908 until 1922 they were in first one and then the other; my father lived in No. 11 during vacations from Cambridge, so did Gwilym; Megan grew up there and Olwen was married from No. 10. I doubt if more laughter has ever been heard there than during this period, for the Lloyd Georges have never been known to take themselves too seriously.

But the pull of Wales remained strong for Nain and by about 1910 she had persuaded LG to build a new house high above Criccieth; it is still there, though sadly no longer owned by the family. Brynawelon ('Hill of the Breezes') became loved by us all, and Nain's magical touch

Brynawelon, Criccieth

with plants – she truly had green fingers – created a beautiful garden. Criccieth is one of those blessed towns that has magically escaped the horrors of development, and as you come over the rise from Pentrefelin and see the sweep of the bay and the castle standing firm on its promontory, it is a sight that lifts the heart.

David Lloyd George's beginnings were far to the south, across the sweep of Cardigan Bay to that still unspoilt countryside that is Pembrokeshire. Here, In June 1864, my great-grandfather (William George) died at the early age of forty-four, leaving two children and a third on the way. He had become a successful headmaster of a school in Manchester (where my grandfather was born) but, dogged by ill-health, returned to farm in his native Pembrokeshire. The Georges had been farmers for many generations at Trecoed, near Fishguard, but the farm William George took was some twenty miles further south, at Bulford near Haverfordwest.

At his death, his widow turned for help to her brother, Richard Lloyd, the village shoemaker at Llanystumdwy. This remarkable man,

David Lloyd George, 1st Earl Lloyd George of Dwyfor

who never married, unhesitatingly took in the entire family, whose possessions, though meagre, were dominated by William George's library of books.

I have often thought that Richard Lloyd's selflessness and devotion to his two nephews for the rest of his life a remarkable example. He took on their education, first teaching himself Latin, Greek and French, and then English Common Law so they could both pass their law examinations and become articled to a firm of solicitors in Portmadoc – and all this while still running a very busy and prosperous shoemaking business, employing five men and entailing much travelling about the area. It was only when the two boys had qualified that he decided to shut up shop and retire to a house in Criccieth. Shortly thereafter, David stood successfully for Parliament and a new world opened for Richard Lloyd. His letters to his nephew David over the next twenty-five years reveal not only his increasing pride in his protégé's parliamentary skills but also his own shrewd understanding of the aims of the Liberal Party and the tactics being adopted to attain these aims. He lived to see his favourite nephew in Downing Street – such a long and arduous journey from the burning of the midnight oil over the law books in the little study of Highgate, Llanystumdwy. My grandfather had long before recognised his debt to his uncle by adding 'Lloyd' to George; his brother William stuck to the simple family surname.

I am often asked, 'How well did you know your grandfather?' Certainly well enough to love him dearly. Long before I was old enough to know that he was in any way different from other men, he had an aura of magic about him. I can readily recall the thrill of excitement of going to see him; he had a beguiling voice – light tenor I suppose, and the most wonderful gurgling laugh which seemed to go on for ages. That, and his twinkling, pale blue eyes, and magnificent leonine head with its flowing mane of white hair, created an amazing image for a small child. Added to which, he genuinely loved children and was always pleased to see us about.

As we grew older he took a keen interest in what we were doing at school and our plans and hopes for the future. I suppose I must have been about nine or ten when I wrote a short and I suspect truly dreadful detective story: Taid's enjoyment of this was amazing; it was just his form, however amateurish. His favourite reading, for relaxation, was detective fiction or 'wild-west' yarns, and he loved the cinema. The library at Churt, a long barrel-vaulted room, was ideal for home movies and these became a regular Saturday-night entertainment.

His attraction for children was as nothing compared with the effect he had on women. As a child one had not of course the slightest inkling of anything 'going on'; if the adults' conversation turned to anything interesting of that sort, which looking back it clearly did fairly often, they switched to Welsh, which, as none of us grandchildren had ever learnt the language, was perfectly maddening. But there always appeared to be a disproportionate number of ladies around the house, and it was clear that this was how Taid liked things. I am leaping ahead in my story, but when at prep-school I happened to be at Churt on two consecutive weekends when Lord Beaverbrook was there, I recall my innocent wonderment that he was on these two occasions accompanied by different ladies.

I think Taid became a different person in the close company of a beautiful woman; if one glances today at photographs of him with, for instance, Sybil Sassoon (later Lady Cholmondeley), he looks far younger than the sixty-year-old he then was, a puckish smile is in place and you can sense that mischief is in the air. As my father once put it, 'with an attractive woman he was as much to be trusted as a Bengal tiger with a gazelle'.

But even later, in 1939, I recall a curious conversation after lunch one day at Churt.

'Owen, how old are you now?'

'Fifteen, Taid.'

'Well I am five times your age but I feel sure I know no more about women than you do now.'

I wish I had had the courage to enquire what rebuff or disappointment had prompted this curious remark, but I think I probably just laughed self-consciously and he changed the subject.

And now it is time I returned to my own beginnings.

CHAPTER 3

Suffolk and Surrey

I have tried in the two preceding chapters to describe the origins and a few salient characteristics of my immediate forebears.

My own childhood, up to the age of about seven, was happy and unremarkable. We lived very comfortably in Springfield, looked after by smiling servants and our devoted Nurse Strike. We often went to the seaside at Aldeburgh, which seemed to be mostly shingle, and once, when I was about four, crossed from Harwich for a short holiday at Knoeke-sur-mer on the Belgian coast. There was a drama there one day when a Belgian boy dug up out of the sand an unexploded German shell. My father gently took it away from him and removed it to safety; the sequel was not so good when the town mayor, heavily bewhiskered, publicly thanked my father, embracing him fervently.

In 1929 my father let the house and we moved up into East Suffolk – to Brandeston, a few miles from Woodbridge, where my McAlpine grandfather had bought him a farm. West Hill, as it was known, became an absorbing passion for him. Unhappily it also absorbed a great deal of my mother's money. But I was fortunately unaware of any such problems and revelled in all that our new home had to offer. It was a beautiful stretch of countryside, totally unspoilt, with large undulating fields that fell away from the house. The land was typical Suffolk clay, and seemed to require vastly expensive drainage systems, though once these were in place, the benefits were considerable.

There were two herds of cattle, Redpolls and Welsh Blacks, as well as some Aryshires to provide us with milk and butter. The two Redpoll bulls, called Cherry and Appleblossom, were woolly, docile creatures, but the Welsh Blacks had a more unpredictable nature. We had Suffolk

West Hill, Brandeston

sheep, of course, Large White pigs and horses of various shapes and sizes, including magnificent Suffolk Punches. I never became a keen horseman but the hours I spent perched high on the backs of those immensely powerful animals, haymaking or harvesting, were magical. My father would take me on an evening tour of the yards and stables, to talk to the animals and give them a handful of something; the stables were always my favourite haunt.

There seemed to be a veritable army of workers to look after everything, some of whom I can remember quite clearly, others only vaguely. Of the latter I recall an overbearing bailiff, with whom my mother had a violent disagreement one hay-making and who left suddenly. There was Norton, who milked the cows and in consequence always seemed to have his cap back-to-front, and Geoffrey, who drove the farm lorry and stoked the boilers and became my special friend later when he used to drive me to and from school. I remember a man called, I think, Tiller, who looked after chickens and sang lustily, and old Fox, our gardener, who had a gammy leg from the war and used to grunt

23

when digging. Then there was Arbon, a wonderful carpenter, always with a beaming smile, whose son Walter became a friend.

Valerie was by this time away at school (she went to St Felix's at Southwold), so I was alone quite a lot, which didn't worry me at all. There was so much to explore with my father's spaniels, secret places that only I knew of, and I lived a Bevis-like life under that great wide Suffolk sky. Nanny Leggatt had taken over from Nurse Strike and gave me simple lessons in the morning-room, which I recall enjoying.

There seemed to be an endless stream of visitors, from both sides of the family. In summertime there were extended picnics in the hayfield or teas in the summerhouse; my Aunt Olwen, who had married Sir Thomas Carey-Evans the same year as my parents were wed, came often with her four children, of whom Robin and Benjy were closest to me in age. Aunt Megan came too: she had just won the Anglesey seat for the Liberals (in 1929) and was at the outset of her political career. We all adored her vivacity and sense of fun and she seemed more like an older sister than an aunt.

Uncle Gwilym and his wife Edna visited too, with their two sons David and William, two more cousins of roughly similar age to myself. Gwilym had also recently entered Parliament as Liberal member for Pembrokeshire.*

There were abundant partridges in East Suffolk in those days and both my father and Gwilym were keen shots. They were joined sometimes by an old friend of my father's, Jack Owain Evans, and his son David, then a rising barrister, who was to play an influential role in my own life. Uncle David, as I thereafter called him, initiated me into shooting, and at the age of seven I shot my first (sitting) rabbit, thus starting a passion that has never left me. Some of us children were frequently enrolled as additional beaters, and learnt the simple lessons of walking in line and keeping quiet. In those very dry summers the

---

* He held that seat until defeated in 1950 by Desmond Donnelly. In 1951 he was elected as the Liberal and Conservative member for North Newcastle upon Tyne, became successively Minister of Fuel and Power, Minister of Food and finally Home Secretary. He was created Viscount Tenby in 1957.

The author with Taid, Brynawelon, 1929

clay would crack into such wide fissures that partridge chicks frequently disappeared into the ground.

I recall one terrible catastrophe. Taid, when Chancellor of the Exchequer in 1914, had called in all the gold in circulation and caused the first pound and ten-shilling notes to be issued. He had given the original ten-shilling note to my father as a souvenir and this was frequently produced to visitors as a curiosity. One Sunday lunch-party at West Hill it had been handed round, and then left on the hall table. Come Monday morning and my mother, short of money to pay the butcher, seized the note without thinking and that was the last time it was ever seen. I have often wondered how much it might be worth today.

Every summer we went on a camping holiday to Minsmere, just south of Dunwich, that sad remnant of a once thriving community which the sea steadily devoured. My father took a site from the local landowner, a Colonel Horsfall, from whom we also had to collect drinking water. Tents were put up and latrines dug; in fact the somewhat military feel was heightened by the presence of disused firing ranges on the heath, where we frequently found empty cartridge-clips from wartime training.

One reached the beach, which was shingly except at low tide, by descending the cliffs on rickety steps, which were frequently destroyed in winter gales. The cliffs themselves were constantly collapsing. Inland, there were endless trails around the mere itself, with bracken over one's head and blackberries galore.

It was a fascinating, wild bit of coastline and I am not surprised that it has since become one of the best bird sanctuaries in Britain, in spite of the looming bulk of Sizewell power station a mile or so away.

We also managed to make a summer visit to Nain at Brynawelon, where the house – by no means a large one – would be bursting with relations. In fact, some of us were often 'farmed out' to a little house on the front. But there would be great games in the garden of Brynawelon, or forgatherings on the beach either at Criccieth or Black Rock, where the sands were much better. If it was August, Taid would be certain to be there too, for he never missed the National Eisteddfod, wherever it was in Wales, and the Thursday of that great festival became, by custom, 'his' day, when he would deliver a great address. To walk with him, down from Brynawelon to the Maes, was to burst with pride, as he was greeted on all sides with affection from old friends and open-mouthed amazement from visitors to the town who suddenly realised that here was the great Wizard in their midst.

But I think he quite quickly got bored there and longed to return either to Churt or Parliament – or both. He was talking one day to J. Hugh Edwards (a fellow Liberal MP and an author of an early life of him) and said, 'John Hugh, you and I, we would do anything for Wales – except live there.'

From Criccieth we would make little excursions – picnics up to the beautiful Cwm Pennant or farther afield – or walk along the back lanes to Llanystumdwy, to hang over the pretty bridge and watch the rushing Dwyfor on its way to the sea. They were happy days.

My McAlpine grandfather had been for some years settled at Knott Park, near Oxshott. My first recollection of a visit there was Christmas 1930. It was a very comfortable, Victorian house, set in typical Surrey rhododendron and Scots-pine country, and seemed to be full of relations, though many of the uncles and aunts had their own houses not far away and just came when summoned. Grandad had never married again after my grandmother died in about 1910 and he loved to have his family about him. He adored bridge and everyone took turns in making up a four at all hours of the day, even in the summerhouse when the weather was warm enough.

One of the permanent residents at Knott Park was Aunt Agnes, my mother's eldest half-sister. She had been married when quite young to a Belgian, the Baron de Belabre, who had disappeared from the scene very quickly with her money, leaving her behind with a young daughter, Yoe. Aunt Agnes took the desertion very badly and appeared to spend a great deal of time in bed, looking sorrowful. I found her rather depressing, though matters were greatly relieved by her companion, Miss Lorraine. This little French person was full of fun and, accompanied everywhere by her Pekinese, adored gambling. She was never happier than when she was playing poker or vingt-et-un with four or

Sir Robert McAlpine at Knott Park

five of us children, but she was frequently roped in to a more sedate game of bridge with Grandad. We all loved her dearly.

There was a ritual every morning of calling to see Grandad in his bedroom. In reply to a knock on the door a firm voice would say 'come'. Although then about eighty-three, he took as keen an interest in everything as ever. About a year later, in 1931, he made a decision that was to have a lasting effect on the McAlpine fortunes. The firm had entered into a joint contract with a leading hotelier, a Mr Gordon, to demolish the old Dorchester House in Park Lane and build a luxury hotel. Six months before completion, Mr Gordon came to see Grandad to explain that as a result of some disastrous business setbacks (in France I believe) he would not be able to complete his side of the contract, which was to provide the finance to fit out and operate the hotel. This was 1931, not a time for banks to lend money on luxury hotels. Grandad summoned his four sons and told them that he had decided to take on the project a hundred per cent. There was a certain amount of dismay expressed and Uncle Tom (Malcolm), I think it was, said, 'Father, you've been a contractor all your life, what on earth do you want to own a hotel for?' to which the old man replied, 'Well, boys, I just feel it may pay off for you one day.'

It certainly did. Though the Dorchester lost money on its catering side until after the war, it provided a magnificent forum from which the McAlpine family could promote their business and was eventually sold to an Arab in the early seventies for nearly ten million pounds.

Knott Park was a very comfortable house and seemed to run like clockwork – though I never discovered whose responsibility the running of it really was. The only members of the staff that I remember clearly after all these years are Charles, the butler, who became a great friend and taught me to ride a bicycle, and Ingles, Grandad's chauffeur, who had waxed moustaches and terrified me. There was also Mcdade, Grandad's valet, a shadowy but kind figure.

The garden was marvellous for children, lots of wandering paths through shrubberies, grass banks to roll down and secret woods to hide in and discuss the grown-ups. There were always dozens of McAlpine cousins; here I first met Christopher and Mary, children of my Uncle

The Dorchester, 1931

Douglas, several years olders than I was, and rather boisterous and alarming. Uncle Douglas (who was my mother's full brother) was the only son not to go into the family business. He studied medicine at the University of Glasgow, served in the navy and took part in the Battle of Jutland; after the war he became an expert on nervous diseases, and was neurological consultant to the army during the Second World War. He also wrote an important study on multiple sclerosis.

The other uncles to be found there were Robert (the eldest son and the one who looked most like Grandad), Willy, Malcolm and Alfred. The last was not a frequent visitor as he ran the Midlands branch of the firm and lived in North Wales; I recall first seeing his son Jimmie, with his habitual friendly grin and chuckling laugh, at Knott Park, when he was in his early twenties. We were to become firm friends.

There had been another uncle, Granville, who died in 1928. From all accounts he was a colourful personality, and immensely popular with all the men on the contracts. But his easy-going ways and fondness for the bottle made his continuance in the firm an embarrassment and he was sent out to Australia, on a generous allowance, the classic remittance man. Unhappily, there was further embarrassment, as Uncle Willy, on a world cruise with his family, called in at Sydney where, to his horror, he saw a large poster outside the principal music-hall announcing, 'Granville McAlpine and his Gorgeous Girls'. Poor Granville was promptly brought home to England but died soon after.

As well as Aunt Agnes, there was Aunt Margaret, next in age to my mother and her closest confidante. She was very attractive, with a most seductive voice. She had married Hugo Chenevix-Trench, but it was not a happy marriage and ended in their separation soon after the First War. Her eldest son, Dick, was a few years older than me, Robin a bit younger.

With these visits to Criccieth and Knott Park my horizons had begun to broaden and the two families came more into focus. But clouds were beginning to darken the sky, and soon after I had been sent away to my first school, the blow fell.

My parents' separation had apparently been foreseen by many of their friends. My father, a most loveable man, was very easy going, enjoyed the good things of life, and from quite an early age drank more than was good for him. My mother, ten years younger, had a very strong personality and a quick temper; as I said earlier, she worshipped her father and was inclined to measure all other men by his high standards. By these criteria she frequently found my father lacking in firmness of purpose. And then there were, undoubtedly, rows over money, which unhappily ran through my father's fingers like water.

But the final break came, as is so often the case, over a third party and the finding of a letter in a discarded coat, a familiar enough story. Needless to say none of this was remotely intelligible to a seven-year-old; the stark fact was my mother had left West Hill and would not be coming back. A pall was cast over my childish spirits and things were never quite the same again.

CHAPTER 4

Hillsbrow, Churt and the Abdication

My early schooldays were not the happiest of times, overshadowed as they were by my parents' separation, and I shall not dwell on them at any length. I was sent first to Eversley, at Southwold, chosen no doubt because of its proximity to Valerie's school, St Felix's, where she had already been for several years. Southwold was, and is, an attractive town and both schools were set back from the cliffs, across a wide common. I would occasionally see Valerie when we were marched on Sundays to the parish church, a lovely building which, with Blythburgh nearby, I have since revisited with pleasure. Our headmaster was called Mr Bee; we had to wear stiff Eton collars daily, the food was appalling and I was miserable. Matters were no better when I was removed after a year or so and sent to a school at Woodbridge, where a Mr Houghton took a sadistic delight in walloping small boys. I suppose I must have learnt something during these years but when I look back the feeling uppermost is one of misery and of not knowing what exactly was happening at home, or why.

In fact, my parents were divorced in 1933, and my mother married David Eifion Evans (Uncle David) the same year. My father married, in 1935, Mrs June Calvé, who had a son and daughter, Roy and Dorothy, who thus became our stepbrother and stepsister and of whom Valerie and I became very fond. Things settled down a bit thereafter, with our holidays being divided between West Hill and Knott Park, though visits to the latter came to an end in 1934 when Grandad died, at the age of eighty-seven. True to form he had built, some six years previously, a vast all-concrete mausoleum in one corner of Cobham Cemetery. It was designed for him by Maxwell Ayrton, the principal architect of

Wembley Stadium, which Grandad had built for the Empire Exhibition in 1924. There are now quite a large number of the second and third generations of the family buried there.

Later that year I went to Hillsbrow, where for the first time I began to enjoy school, made real friends and started to learn properly and take responsibility. This prep school in Surrey had been started only ten years before by G. D. Seale, a remarkable man with a great gift for leadership and a true understanding of how schoolboys' minds work. He was a first-class cricketer, had played for Hampshire, and if he had a fault it was that games tended sometimes to take priority over lessons, which was no hardship for us. Jack Hobbs was a lifelong friend of his and came down every summer to do some coaching; he had a great twinkle and gave us all immense encouragement with bat and ball. Alas, his talents were largely wasted on me and I never rose to great heights. Boxing and rugger were more to my taste, and I had some success in both.

Among my contemporaries was Gordon Richards's son, and the great jockey was often to be seen, a small stocky figure, exuding confidence though in fact very shy. The two Rickaby brothers, famous jockeys too, but under National Hunt rules, had also been at Hillsbrow a few years earlier.

The school had the happiest of atmospheres, there was no bullying, and parents were encouraged to visit and take out their sons at almost any time. In May 1935, I was allowed two nights in London to watch the celebration of the Silver Jubilee of George V and Queen Mary. My mother and Uncle David had by then moved to a flat in Carlisle Mansions. Uncle David and I made our way to some offices belonging to a friend of his in Ludgate Hill, a superb viewing position just a hundred yards from St Paul's Cathedral where the service was held. It was a boiling hot day but I hardly left the balcony for a minute, watching the contingents of troops taking up position, the build-up of the procession and the climax when the King and Queen came up the hill in an open carriage to thunderous cheers. There was then an hour or so to wait while the service took place and then they reappeared at the great doorway of St Paul's and acknowledged the cheers of the crowds. The Sovereign's Escort moved off, I again gazed down at the royal couple on their return journey, and watched fascinated as various other dignitaries passed by. The Emperor of Abyssinia, Haile Selassie, alone in an open landau, seemed to get a tremendous ovation.

During all this time I had seen remarkably little of Uncle David, who appeared to find the attractions of the hospitality within greater than the processions outside; when it was time to move off he was extremely jovial but a trifle unsteady on his feet, and we nearly succeeded in being run down by my own grandparents in their powder-blue Rolls-Royce. Eventually we got on a District Line train, where there was a good deal of singing – in which Uncle David joined – and back to the flat where he promptly went to bed. My mother's only comment was that 'he had had too much sun'. I remember thinking this odd, as it was the one thing he hadn't had much of.

Mr Seale used often to take the entire school to either Lord's or the Oval, where we saw some wonderful cricket; Wally Hammond and Hardstaff batting, Verity and Ken Farnes bowling and little Eddy Paynter fielding are among the clear images that I recall.

Hillsbrow was on a ridge, above Redhill (not far from Nutfield where my Uncle Willy McAlpine then lived). One night in 1936, we were all in bed when an extraordinary glow in the sky to the north was seen. This was the Crystal Palace, burnt to the ground overnight.

It was during these years (1935–8) that I was most frequently at Churt; Taid was still at the height of his intellectual powers, churning out ideas such as his 'New Deal' for the 1935 election campaign, and there was a constant stream of high-powered visitors to the house, such as Churchill, Beaverbrook and H. G. Wells. I was often banished from the dining-room if there was insufficient room (it was remarkably small) and would lunch with Miss Frances Stevenson in her room. She was always kind and gentle in manner and I simply accepted her then as one of the more important members of Taid's staff. It was to be several more years before I learnt that her role in his life was a great deal more demanding.

Bron-y-de (meaning 'Slope of the South'), the house at Churt, had been built by the architect Philip Tilden in 1922/3 to Taid's specification, on land he had purchased the previous year. The site was a splendid

The library, Churt. The mural by Johnny Churchill

one, with views to the Devil's Jumps and distant Hampshire. Tilden, in his autobiography *True Remembrances,* describes well the many alterations and additions that were demanded by his client, but having worked for Churchill at Chartwell, he knew how to accept them with equanimity.

The main feature of the house was the library, which ran the whole length of the building and had a high barrel-vaulted ceiling; at one end there was a striking semi-circular mural of the Bay of Rapallo. This had been done by Johnny Churchill, Winston's nephew and a talented painter, who had included in the painting his very attractive wife, seated to the left holding a document which represented the Treaty of Rapallo.

Thousands of books, including Taid's state papers beautifully bound in leather, lined the walls, and in large glass cabinets were the many freedoms that he had received. Of these the one that always fascinated me the most was from Criccieth, a beautifully modelled replica in silver of the castle on its mound. On the grand piano and on various tables

*Churt, 1935 – at back Megan and David; front Dick, the author, Nain,
Olwen, Edna, Gwilym, Margie, Taid, Valerie, Tom*

were countless photographs of World War I personalities, such as Foch,
Clemenceau, Woodrow Wilson, Smuts and Asquith, to be joined later
by ones of Hitler and Mussolini.* It was in this room that Taid wrote the
greater part of his *War Memoirs*, sitting in his wing chair to the right of
the huge open fire. Here too he would have an instant nap after lunch,
with a wild-west story still firmly clenched in his hand; I once
inadvertently woke him from such a sleep and was firmly dismissed
with a vigorous expletive.

The room opened out at the far end into a sun-room, which in turn
opened on to the garden where a long double border led down to the
orchards. Taid had originally bought sixty acres but over the years
added more land so that he eventually had close on eight hundred
acres, a large part of which was commercial orchards or soft fruit. A lot
of the land was sandy scrub when he acquired it: pigs were first allowed
the run of the place, rooting up and manuring as they went. But, always

* The last two now repose, more appropriately in my view, in the smallest room
  of my home in Pembrokeshire.

*Churt, the small sitting-room with portrait of Richard Lloyd by
Philip de Lazlo*

impatient for results, he brought in a vastly expensive machine called a
Giro-tiller to do the job more quickly than the pigs.

In due course, a shortage of water to irrigate such a large area of fruit
became a problem and an old Scottish lady, Mrs Wyllie, a water diviner,
was brought in to help. She succeeded brilliantly and an artesian well
was duly sunk which was soon producing three hundred thousand
gallons a day. A large building was constructed for sorting and packing
the apples and keeping them at the right temperature, after which they
were dispatched to Harrods and other up-market outlets, stamped
'product of Bron-y-de Farms'.

Bees became another of Taid's enthusiasms, to the extent that his
Welsh secretary, Miss Ann Parry, became additionally keeper of the
bees. The honey was superb and won prizes regularly. We all benefited
hugely from these enterprises and would return to school laden with
honey, jam, apples, etc.

Christmas at Churt

What the cost of all this must have been I shudder to think; certainly it could not have been managed without regular dips into the 'Lloyd George Political Fund'. The photograph on p. 39, taken on Armistice Day 1935, gives some idea of the number of men employed then.

Christmases at Churt were splendid occasions. A large tree in the library with presents piled high; all the children of everyone who worked on the place came to a huge tea and each received a present, after which there would be games or a film show with George Dyer the chauffeur at the projector. Taid adored to have children about him and had a magical touch with them, which I have already described.

He also loved dogs and over the years owned a great many. Before I was born, and while he was still Prime Minister, he owned a black chow bitch called Chong, a present from Sir Philip Sassoon; she was reputed to lie outside the cabinet room and know exactly who was talking, be it Curzon, Churchill or her beloved master. Bang was

38

Armistice Day, Churt, 1935

another chow, a red one, whom I remember well and who once saw off a burglar at Addison Road. And then there was Grock, a wire-haired fox terrier and a great little character who appears in the photograph taken at Churt on p. 36.

I have already referred to Taid's clumsiness with his hands and inability to do up things like shoelaces; nevertheless he had a strong streak of vanity and was always elegantly dressed, generally in a pale blue suit that matched the colour of his eyes, a dashing bow tie, his gold pince-nez dangling from a silk ribbon about his neck, and one of many favourite hats which still allowed full rein to his abundant silvery white hair. To cap it all, and as a gift to cartoonists, he never went outside (in the country) without his flowing black cloak.

In London, from his earliest days as an MP when money was very tight, he had always been immaculately turned out, and now, in his maturity as an elder statesman, he was an imposing, indeed dramatic, figure in morning coat and shining top-hat.

A figure who was to become a firm friend was A. J. Sylvester, Taid's principal private secretary from 1923 until his death. AJ (as he was always known in the family) had an amazing career. Born in 1889 to a farming family in Staffordshire, he won an international shorthand competition and joined the Civil Service before the First World War, travelling to India in 1912–13 as assistant reporter for the Royal Commission on Public Services. Soon after war broke out he became secretary to Hankey, and as a result, in 1915, was the first shorthand writer ever to take a note of a cabinet committee. He was Taid's secretary first in 1921, and, after he fell from office in 1922, remained at No. 10, first as secretary to Bonar Law and then Baldwin, before returning to LG. Thereafter he never left his side and I doubt if any man in public life ever

Port Lympne, 1921 – from left unknown, Lord Riddell, Phillip Kerr, Philip Sassoon, unknown, unknown, M. Barthelot, Lord Vansittart, Lloyd George, Lady Rocksavage, Camerlynch (interpreter), M. Briand, AJ, Captain Burgess

Lloyd George at Chequers in 1921, with Briand and Foch;
Philip Sasson is in the background.

had a more conscientious or devoted secretary. His duties were far-ranging; not only did he run the private office (at Thames House at the time of which I am writing) where there was a staff of twenty, but he also virtually ran his private life too, making travel arrangements here and abroad, interviewing countless people to check facts for the *War Memoirs* and at the same time playing diplomat between various family members. He had a prodigious capacity for work, an inability to take 'no' for an answer and unswerving loyalty to his chief. At the same time he always seemed to me the same smiling, cheerful person, invariably glad to see me; my earliest recollection of AJ is, as a very small boy, clutching his hand as we threaded the labyrinth of Westminster on the way to Taid's room. 'Now, Mr Sylvester will look after you,' and he always did.

In 1934 my mother bought about forty acres of the old Lythe Hill estate, just south of Haslemere, on the Surrey/Sussex boundary and adjoining Blackdown, which had been one of the earliest National Trust acquisitions. It was approached along Tennyson's Lane, so called because it led to Aldworth, for many years the home of the erstwhile Poet Laureate. Here he wrote, in a tribute to General Hamley:

> You came, and look'd and loved the view
> Long-known and loved by me,
> Green Sussex fading into blue
> With one gray glimpse of sea.

It was indeed possible to see the sea, on a clear day, at a distance of nearly thirty miles, so this was not poetic licence. Tennyson had of course died over forty years before and at the time of which I am writing Aldworth belonged to the Gaekwar of Baroda.

My mother planned a house on a magnificent site, eight hundred feet up. When the position was more or less chosen I was sent up a large Douglas fir to check that the view was as good as hoped for. It was, and work commenced later that year; during the construction she and Uncle David spent weekends in Owlden, a four-hundred-year-old cottage on the property and a reputed base for smugglers in the eighteenth century. There was of course no electricity, telephone or indeed mains of any sort: candles and paraffin lamps and huge log fires

Owlswood, Blackdown

that never went out were our main comforts, and I loved every minute of it. The woods were a haven for abundant bird-life. I found several badger sets and spent hours watching them, and there were snakes such as I have never seen since. I once watched a green grass snake moving over some logs and am prepared to swear it was six feet long. Adders abounded, and my mother's spaniel got bitten once.

The house, to be called Owlswood, came on rapidly and proved a great success. We cleared huge areas of ponticum rhododendron and my mother started laying out what became quite an extensive garden. She had only one helper, Kelsey, who subsequently took on milking the few cows she acquired and feeding the pigs, chickens and geese, as well as gardening and helping in the house.

Uncle David was at this time building up a considerable reputation as a barrister. Although he was nineteen years my senior, he and I soon became fast friends and I owe him a great deal, for he introduced me to so many interests, then and later, and always provided a sympathetic ear for my particular anxiety of the moment. We spent many happy hours hacking our way through the overgrown paths, having enormous bonfires and sawing up logs with a cross-cut; happy days indeed.

For several years we took, in the summer, a small house called Bellevue Farm, at Llangennith, on the Gower coast, with its many rocky headlands and its long sweep of sands culminating in the Worm's Head. We would spend idyllic days on the beach at Broughton Bay or Burry Holms, with cricket on the sands and swimming in the Blue Pool. This is a part of Wales that has, thank goodness, been very well protected and looks now much as it did fifty years ago.

Meanwhile, at West Hill, things were becoming less happy. Although the farm seemed to prosper, and my father had started an extensive day-old chicken business as an additional outlet, he had simultaneously made a rash plunge into the house-building field. This was 1935/6 and houses were certainly in demand, especially by the larger authorities such as Glasgow, Leeds and Birmingham. To these, and other cities, my father made frequent visits on behalf of the company, since the family name undoubtedly helped oil the wheels. Unfortunately, the principal of the firm, a Mr Whatling, turned out to be a rogue, and although I cannot recall the precise facts, he was sent to gaol for nine months as a result. My father had pledged a considerable sum of money to the firm, this was called in, the firm went into liquidation and by 1937 West Hill had to be sold. I believe the land fetched about ten pounds per acre. It was heartbreaking for him, as well as for June and all of us; we moved back to Springfield, which he still owned, until that too had to be sold, just before the war, and he and June moved to a flat in London. He had a first-rate brain, genuine love and knowledge of the land and livestock, was adored by everyone who ever did a day's work for him, but was a hopeless judge of his fellow men and very easily led and used by others. Sadly, he had also, from the end of the war, over-indulged in the hard stuff and after the catastrophe that I have just described it was largely a downhill road.

Taid and Nain's London home at this time was 2 Addison Road, a solid, comfortable house with a large garden that had a tennis court and greenhouses. Valerie and Margie (Carey-Evans) had a joint coming-out dance there in the summer of 1936, when they were both eighteen, but I was of course too young to be included. I did, however, stay there for two nights during that summer when my grandparents gave an evening reception to which the King (Edward VIII) came. My father brought me up and my main recollection is of a quite small but infinitely friendly and smiling person who chatted to me for a few minutes. A few months later, at Hillsbrow, towards the end of the Michaelmas term, we were all allowed to come from our dormitories one evening and sit on the staircase to listen to the abdication broadcast on Mr Seale's wireless. Few of us boys had much idea what had precipitated this crisis (it had only 'broken' in the papers nine days before) and it was only later that I became aware of my family's anguish over the King's dilemma. As a very young Prince of Wales he had come to 11 Downing Street in 1910, as my father described:

> For several months, two or three evenings each week, the youthful heir to the throne would come to No 11 for his coaching. From the time he entered the house until he left it he heard very little English spoken. (There was nothing unusual about this, Welsh being the only language ever used by any of us when we were *en famille*.) But it must have been a trying experience for the youngster – at least for the first few sessions. As I have already said, there was a definite streak of the thespian in my father in those days. He enjoyed nothing better than to set the stage for a theatrical affect, and the coming of his distinquished pupil afforded an unparalleled opportunity that he was not slow to grasp.
>
> The Prince, haltingly at first, but ever improving, enunciated his Welsh sentences with a very clear boyish voice – he was only fifteen at the time.
>
> As these evenings continued over a period of several months we all came to know our scholar, and to like him tremendously. That affection, so far as I am concerned, was complemented by a great admiration for the young man. I know my mother's admiration of him matched mine, and certainly he held an especially warm corner in her capacious heart. Further, I can speak for her as well as myself when I say that nothing that subsequently transpired lessened our admiration and affection for him an iota.

These lessons in Welsh were, of course, a preparation for the Prince of Wales's investiture which took place on 13 July 1911. Taid, as Constable of Caernarvon Castle was responsible for all the elaborate arrangements; indeed it had been he who had begged the King to revive the long-dormant ceremony. Everything went off splendidly (not a cloud in the sky – unlike 1969), but it was an undoubted ordeal for a sixteen-year-old boy, and my father long held to a theory that that day may have decided him never to face a coronation.

Be that as it may, the quotation given above amply demonstrates the long-standing affection that the family felt for Edward VIII. As matters turned out, Taid was on holiday in Jamaica at the time of the abdication, and although he made immediate arrangements to return when he was alerted by cable to the crisis, the affair had been resolved before he could sail. What difference might it have made had he been in London and able to intervene? Very little in my view. Churchill (equally sympathetic to the King) was howled down in the Commons when he pleaded for delay before a final decision was reached; he and Taid together might have made Baldwin's task more difficult but the eventual outcome was surely never in doubt.

Reverting for a moment to the 1911 Investiture, I have in my possession a letter from Lord Penrhyn's solicitors to Taid, dated 7 November 1910, which clearly indicates that negotiations had reached a fairly advanced stage for the purchase, on behalf of the Prince of Wales, of a part of the Penrhyn estate. It included Penrhyn Park, some seven hundred acres with salmon fishing on the River Ogwen and shooting rights. There is nothing to indicate why these negotiations came to an end, and I only bring the matter into my story for the reason that I feel very sad that the present Prince of Wales has no home in the principality.

The following May (1937), Valerie and I watched the Coronation processions from a stand in Parliament Square, a wonderful viewpoint as we were no distance from the Abbey. A. J. Sylvester shepherded us to our seats and when all was over collected us so that we could rejoin our grandparents who had been at the ceremony. My recollection of this part of the proceedings is that there was a severe snarling-up of the traffic arrangements and it seemed to take hours. I recall standing next to Taid at the top of the steps in St Stephen's Hall (they must have crossed the road from the Abbey) surrounded by splendidly attired ladies and gentlemen. At last we got into the Rolls (driven I think by Weller, Nain's chauffeur, not Dyer), for the return to Addison Road. Progress was very slow and not improved by the fact that every few yards we were mobbed by excited crowds who recognised Taid. At one point an old workman, somewhat inebriated, climbed into the car and insisted on shaking hands with us all. It was a very exhilarating experience.

Now in my last year at Hillsbrow, I was made head boy. My boxing had improved, and I became quite a useful member of the rugger fifteen, playing on the wing, but it was cricket that took pride of place in the school year. Fathers' matches were always a high spot, as they coincided with half-term when we had a 'leave-out' until the Monday evening; I never succeeded in persuading my own parent to take part, even though he was quite a respectable left-handed batsman.

The school chapel was pressed into use for the many lectures and the like that we had arranged for us, especially in the winter. I recall Captain Knight coming with his golden eagle (called, I think, Ramsey) and allowing the bird to fly low over our heads. Another regular visitor was Grey Owl, the Red Indian chief, who told us fascinating tales of the wilder parts of North America. Alas, I heard long afterwards that he was a complete fake and had in fact been born in England.

The school magazine for 1938 has an entry by a contemporary, Michael Trinick:

On Monday 16 May, Mr Seale very kindly took all those who had played in last year's First Eleven for a surprise visit to Lord's, to see the Australians play the MCC.

Mr Seale found us very good seats in the front row, and when the game started we were all excited because Bradman was in. Soon, unfortunately, he was out, caught marvellously by the MCC captain at cover point for 278. The Australians were eventually out for 502. At lunchtime our provisions were augmented by Mr Chudley, who arrived lugging along a huge parcel of sandwiches and cakes.

The MCC continued after lunch, but were out for 214. After tea they followed on till they were 43 for one wicket. At the tea interval we went out and looked at the pitch where a great hole had been made by the fast bowler Smith.

About 6.15 we left, at the kind invitation of Major Lloyd George, for his flat nearby, where he filled us up with cakes and drinks. Major Lloyd George showed us the first gun ever made during the War in government factories. It seemed very heavy and when Chudley did sentry-go with it he nearly collapsed.*

This, I think, gives an accurate flavour of the very happy life we had at Hillsbrow, a school which sadly came to an end in the late forties, following Mr Seale's death.

I had passed my common entrance exam for Oundle and in September 1938 started a new chapter of my life there.

---

* This rifle was the first Enfield.303 manufactured by the Winchester Repeating Arms Company in America for Britain in 1916, with a serial number W1, and was presented to my grandfather, a plaque on the butt recording the event. In 1983 I presented it to the Army Museum.

CHAPTER 5

Oundle

Oundle is an attractive small town in the Northamptonshire country-side, with an abundance of sixteenth- and seventeenth-century houses, many roofed in the local slate, called Collyweston, and dominated by the church of St Peter's, whose tall spire can be seen from far away. There is (or was) a thriving boat-building business and the River Nene skirts the lower part of the town. Barnwell, home of the Duke of Gloucester, is two miles away, also Lilford Hall, home of the great naturalist, and, to the north, Fotheringay Castle, the prison house of Mary Queen of Scots, where she was executed in 1587. The country-side is totally rural and blessedly unspoilt.

The school had been founded in 1556 by Sir William Laxton, but it was not until the late nineteenth century that it started to expand and acquire its reputation, unrivalled among other public schools, for teaching the sciences and engineering. This was solely due to a remarkable headmaster, F. W. Sanderson, who from his appointment in 1892 until his sudden death thirty years later, persuaded the Grocers' Company, the governing body, to pour money into the building of physics and chemistry laboratories, engineering workshops, a foundry, woodworking shops and countless other facilities. Sanderson was also a close friend of H. G. Wells, who shared his belief in offering boys a wider choice than classics and languages and actively encouraged him in his efforts.

By the time I arrived, Sanderson's successor, Dr Fisher, had been headmaster for some years; he too had a scientific background, his speciality being chemistry. He was credited, by his pupils at least, with having invented mustard gas during the First War. Whether it was true

49

or not, we rejoiced in the fable, especially as in all other respects 'Bud' Fisher was singularly unmartial. I always got on well with him, on the rare occasions that our paths crossed; his benevolence to me may have had something to do with the fact that he and Mrs Fisher had for many years taken their summer holidays at Harlech, and become great friends of Nain, who for some reason used to send them Eccles cakes.

I do not know exactly how or when the choice of Oundle was made for me but I am fairly certain that it was my mother's doing; I had certainly expressed an early interest in civil engineering and there was the possibility of my joining the family firm of McAlpine's, for which the school would provide a good grounding, even if I did not go on to Cambridge, as my father certainly wished. Two of my McAlpine cousins, Edwin and Malcolm (D.), had already been educated at Oundle. In any event it was my mother who was going to be paying the fees, as my other parent was certainly in no position to do so.

I arrived at Oundle at the height of the Munich Crisis (15–30 September 1938) but cannot say that it worried me unduly; my apprehension was reserved for what lay ahead in terms of a new, and far larger, school. As things turned out I settled in fairly easily, in spite of some inevitable homesickness. I was in Grafton, one of the eleven houses that made up the school, which as well as occupying quite a chunk of the old town, spread outwards into the countryside. Grafton was one of those houses, purpose-built, which had been added at the turn of the century when the great expansion of the school under Sanderson took place; it was actually divided so that another house, Sydney, adjoined. It was really pretty basic, with dining-room, changing-room, common-room and rows of studies on the ground floor, and dormitories, washing facilities and sick-room above. Lavatory facilities were Spartan and housed in an outdoor building a few yards from the back door; one of the least alluring of a fag's duties involved sitting for ten minutes or so on an ice-cold seat to thaw it out for his fag-master's subsequent visit.

Some of the other houses, especially those like Laundimer, were in attractive period houses in the town, and School House was the grandest, incorporating the Fishers' quarters (they had six children, of whom at least two taught at Oundle).

My housemaster was Alan Cutcliffe, a strong character if ever there was one. Short and stocky, he was an excellent oar and helped to coach the school eight, as well as refereeing rugger matches and teaching classics into the bargain. He was a strict disciplinarian, but achieved his ends more by force of character than open chastisement, though he was not averse to giving a beating when one was merited. Although he had lost two fingers of one hand (I now forget which) when working as a lumberjack in Canada, he was very agile; his nickname of 'Cutie' was really very unsuitable, there was nothing remotely 'twee' about him and we all held him in great respect. His assistant at Grafton was one 'Teddy' de Ville, who had been an aviator, taught science and was equally popular.

Some of the other masters that I encountered were more forbidding, or at any rate, remote. King (of New House) and Nightingale, who commanded the Corps, were Olympian figures of uncertain temper; Cordukes taught languages and was generally considered easy-going; Mr Priestman had School House, was adjutant of the Corps and enjoyed putting on uniform enormously; Willie Boggs was chaplain and delivered incredibly dull sermons; his assistant, Cullingford, subsequently became padre to 1st Battalion Welsh Guards; and then of course there was dear Arthur Marshall, of BBC fame, who tried to teach me French but who kept us in fits of laughter. One could locate his class anywhere in the school from the gales of laughter that shook the windows.

But all of the foregoing were unknown to me in my early days there, when I struggled – as generations of schoolboys have done – to be in the right place at the right time with the proper books and equipment. The whole school, six hundred of us, assembled each morning for prayers in school hall, when important announcements were made. (In a year or so, these would include names of boys killed in action or awarded decorations.) The day would then unfold to a pattern of varying periods, lunch, organised games, tea, prep – the usual school routine. I had passed into the form below Remove and coped reasonably well that first term; later I got slack and failed the School Certificate at my first attempt.

On Sundays we all wore straw boaters, winter or summer, and trooped into the school chapel, just across from Grafton. A striking feature at the entrance was a sculpture, by Katherine Scott, of the naked boy Samuel – 'Here am I, send me' – the model for which had been her son Peter Scott. He subsequently entered the school and, I was told, received a lot of chaffing about his anatomical details.

I had played a fair amount of rugger at Hillsbrow and was soon competent enough to take part in junior house matches. I also carried on with my boxing. Training for this was done in a small, scruffy building behind the chapel and supervised by one Syd Barnes, a caricature of an old-time bruiser, who had been army heavyweight champion. A man of few words, he nevertheless gave me much encouragement and taught me a great deal, with the result that over the next three years I won my weight regularly, boxed for the school frequently and got my school colours when I was sixteen. Charles Simeons, who was head of Grafton and school heavyweight champion, kept me at it, I recall. It is the only sport I can remotely claim to have been good at; funnily enough it has a similarity to public speaking, which I loathe. Terrible foreboding before, but, once you are launched in the ring and the bell goes, total concentration on beating the other fellow. I never lost a fight, either at Oundle or in the army. The great thing about boxing is that the training for it is so exacting that, as Syd used to say, 'if you're fit to box you're fit for anything'.

The end of that first term came round and I recall walking to the station with my suitcase in the early dark, so cold that my hand froze to the handle. That Christmas (1938) was a white one; we were in the new house on Blackdown and the hills were deep in snow. Aunt Margaret (my mother's sister) had taken a house a few miles away so we saw a lot of my cousins Dick and Robin Trench.

Dick was about seventeen, at Charterhouse, tall, very self-assured and amusing. He joined the RAF a year later as a bomber pilot and was killed in 1942.

Valerie had gone up to Oxford two years before and was at St Hilda's, which she seemed to be enjoying to the full. As a fourteen-year-old brother I probably failed to realise what a very attractive sister I had; her contemporaries were more appreciative.

I didn't see Taid during those holidays but his Christmas present was

Oundle boxing team, 1940 (the author front right)

a set of Conan Doyle's historical novels, *Rodney Stone, Adventures of Brigadier Gerard*, etc. At about this time I became a voracious reader, encouraged by Uncle David, and my appetite ranged widely, from the Waverley Novels to John Buchan and Sapper and back to Dickens.

During 1939 I settled happily to life at Oundle, making friends and taking advantage of the wide variety of activities there. After a year of fagging, I shared a study with R. P. (Freddie) Dixon and Gavin Caldwell-Smith. Other contemporaries in Grafton were Dick Bowser, John Glennie and one Molesworth, always known as the Admiral since he seemed determined on a naval career. We were a pretty rowdy lot, I suppose, but generally avoided getting into serious trouble. Looking back I am amazed at the amount we smoked, surreptitiously of course. I had started smoking at Hillsbrow (after parents came to tea at cricket matches there were always dozens of half-smoked cigarettes about) and enjoyed it. Kipling describes the illicit smoking by boys so accurately in

Stalky & Co. Later, in the army, anyone who didn't use tobacco was almost thought a bit odd, and during training the habitual command was, 'Right, fall out for a smoke.' I wonder what happens today.

My two Carey-Evans cousins, Robin and Benjy, were both in School House; we bumped into each other occasionally during school and when Aunt Olwen and Uncle Tom came down to take them out I was always included, which was very good of them. The Talbot, an early seventeenth-century coaching inn, was where parents usually stayed, and where we would tuck into large lunches and teas.

I adored Uncle Tom. He had spent a lot of his younger days in India, and indeed after their marriage, he and Aunt Olwen were out there for several years when he was surgeon to the Viceroy, Lord Reading. (Their second daughter, Eluned, was born in India.) Uncle Tom had been a keen big-game hunter and could tell thrilling tales of tiger shoots and stalking bears. At the time of which I write he was in charge of Hammersmith Hospital, and the family lived in Ducane Road, where I often stayed.

Among the several things for which I am grateful to Oundle I rate highly my introduction to music. Every year the school would perform a major oratorical work, such as Handel's *Messiah*, the *Christmas Oratorio* or Haydn's *Creation*. About a third of the school were choir; you had to be really tone deaf to be excluded, though Benjy achieved this. During the Michaelmas term we would work steadily through one of these great works, under the enthusiastic but highly critical eye of the music master J. A. Tatam and in company with the very substantial school orchestra. At last, after a full-length rehearsal, the final performance took place and was frequently broadcast, with well-known soloists from the BBC taking part and with many parents and outside guests in the audience. It was a thrilling experience and started me on a lifelong love of classical music.

One thing I regret in retrospect is that I didn't opt to row instead of playing cricket, at which I never succeeded in distinguishing myself. Oundle had, by the 1930s, become a very formidable rowing school, and there were few years when the Cambridge eight failed to contain one, or even two, Oundelians. The River Nene afforded a splendid challenge, and when it flooded, which was a regular occurrence, one could row across half the county.

In August 1939 my mother, David and I drove to the west coast of Scotland on holiday and at Oban chartered a small boat, with one hand, intending to cruise around the Western Isles. This was something my mother had been planning to do for years, partly because as a child she had spent so many happy days on Grandad's yatch based on the Clyde. Sadly by the time we had gone on one or two excursions the news from Europe was becoming more and more ominous and our cruise had to be aborted.

Back at school, after war had been declared, air-raid shelters were being built for every house and we all had to spend so many hours every week digging a vegetable allotment; the Corps took on a more serious aspect. The black-out was strictly observed.

My father rejoined the army, and was soon at the War Office, attached to the Quartermaster General's Department; he came down to take me out one Saturday, resplendent in uniform. In the Talbot before lunch he took me aside and, explaining that he had come without any money, asked how much I had in my PO savings book. I had about seven pounds, so I ran up to Grafton and collected it, down to the Post Office and withdrew the three pounds maximum one was then allowed and handed it over. A few minutes later I heard him in jolly fettle with Uncle Tom (who was down also) and others in the bar buying drinks all round; and I never saw my three pounds again! His appointment was a blessing in disguise, at any rate for a time, as it gave him a regular job and an assured income which was badly needed; life in London was not always the happiest arrangement for him.

Taid's attitude to the war during the autumn of 1939 was strangely ambivalent. At the outbreak of hostilities he pledged full support to the government in a short speech to the Commons, recalling his experience in the 1914–18 War, and saying, 'We will do it again.' But by October, with Poland overrun, Russia to all appearances allied to Germany and no action as yet in the West, he was in no doubt that the door should be left open for an international conference, organised by non-aligned countries (including the USA), to try and avert all-out war. He was severely criticised in many quarters for what was seen as a negative and possibly defeatist attitude, but I am certain that he acted from the fear that there was about to be a repetition of the appalling carnage in the earlier conflict; added to which, it was his contention that we were now, with the dominions at our side, in a totally different and stronger position than we had been at the time of Munich. He was writing every week in the *Sunday Pictorial*, and expressed his views very forcibly, as always.

Valerie had got a good degree at Oxford and was now working for Sir William Beveridge on his massive and important report. At about the same time she had met, and fallen in love with, Goronwy Daniel, a don who was an exact contemporary of Harold Wilson at Jesus College. Wilson said to him one day, 'Goronwy, you ought to meet Miss Lloyd George, she's a bit of all right.' Goronwy did, and agreed totally. I have since been told that the story is apocryphal, but it has the ring of truth to me, and shows that, whatever one may think of his later career, Harold Wilson's judgement during his Oxford days was impeccable.

They were engaged by Christmas and I vividly recall Valerie bringing Goronwy to stay at Owlswood for the first time. He was politically very far to the left in those days and Uncle David, even though he had stood as a Liberal candidate in 1929, was now staunchly right-wing. The conversation at dinner became very heated, much to poor Valerie's dismay, and my mother had to calm the two antagonists down. After that initial hiccup all went swimmingly and they were married at Headington the following March.

By April the pace of events quickened in Europe and the nine o'clock news on the radio became the most gripping moment of the day. On the 9th the Germans occupied Copenhagen and then invaded Norway, to which we responded by sending a badly prepared expeditionary force which had to make an ignominious withdrawal two weeks later. The great 'Norway' debate on 7 and 8 May provided Taid with the opportunity to make what was to prove his last great intervention in the affairs of the nation, though he nearly missed it. He had gone to his room in the Commons while Chamberlain was speaking and it was Megan who flew, almost literally, down the corridors to tell him that the Prime Minister had just spoken of 'sacrifice'. 'Tada, you must speak,' she said. He did, including the words, ' . . . I say solemnly that the Prime Minister should give an example of sacrifice, because there is nothing that can contribute more to victory in this war than that he should sacrifice the seals of office.'

Chamberlain resigned and on 10 May Churchill succeeded him. During that extraordinary summer we listened to all Churchill's speeches on our study radio, becoming accustomed to that amazing voice, exhorting us to be of good cheer when, after Dunkirk, things seemed black indeed. We also listened to Hitler, ranting away at inordinate length. Even in a relatively isolated community such as Oundle was we became aware of the desperate situation Britain was in, and yet a curious calm seemed to have settled on the country once it was clear that we were alone. All plans for the future were off, older boys were putting their names down for one or other of the services and many had already left to join up; older brothers had been posted missing, some killed. The Corps took on a more realistic role and fearsome regular officers descended on the school to give pep talks; the Local Defence Volunteers (forerunner of the Home Guard) were formed, and were to be seen patrolling the railway line, and pill boxes were constructed in curious places.

Taid's weekly article for the *Sunday Pictorial* on 21 July was headlined WE WILL WIN THROUGH and was a robust essay on the determination of the British people to withstand anything Hitler could throw at us. Nevertheless, he was still not personally prepared to join in the fight; a month before, Churchill had formally offered him a seat in the cabinet, with a role that he himself could choose, but he turned it down, ostensibly because he refused to serve with Chamberlain. Beaverbrook, Boothby, Garvin and others all tried their best to persuade him, but without success.

AJ recorded in his diary (14 June),

The other day LG received a firm and definite offer to go into the cabinet from Winston, Neville Chamberlain having concurred in the suggestion. I was against LG going in at the time he wrote to Winston, but now the situation has deteriorated so much that it is vital that LG should be inside. He has such vision, and I have such faith in him still. Beaverbrook has been trying to induce LG to accept. Frances and I have both impressed upon him the importance of his accepting. But he now sticks his toes in and says: 'I won't go in with this crowd,' which means with Neville.*

And so this strange summer wore on. A few bombs were dropped at Biggin, a mile or so away, but otherwise Oundle was undisturbed, and at the end of July we dispersed for the holidays. In the early part of August I saw dog-fights taking place regularly high over Blackdown and on one occasion watched a German bomber spiralling to the ground; twenty minutes hard pedalling on my bike and I reached the scene – an enormous crater and bits of plane and enemy airmen scattered around.

Uncle David had become a reservist in 1938 and was now commissioned with the rank of captain, serving in Northern Ireland, so that my mother was alone at Owlswood. An invitation came from her brother Alfred (McAlpine) to stay for a few weeks at Llanarmon, where he had an estate, and to bring me as well. It turned out to be a never-forgotten holiday for me, and had a decisive effect on my subsequent career.

Llanarmon Dyffryn Ceiriog (the church of St Garmon in the Vale of the Ceiriog) to give it its full name, lies some twelve miles to the west of Chirk, in old Denbighshire, almost at the head of a narrow, twisting valley. In the whitewashed farmhouse, known as Pen y Bryn, high on the north side of this valley, was born in 1832 the poet John Ceiriog Hughes, author of the lovely *Bugeilio'r Gwenith Gwyn*, and many other beautiful songs and poems, and an acclaimed winner at many an Eisteddfod. The village is tiny, with a small cluster of houses, the church and post-office, and one hotel – in the days of which I am speaking, the West Arms.

For many years the Llanarmon estate, famed for its exceptionally high pheasants, was owned by the Cornwallis-West† family, who had let it on

---

* A. J. Sylvester, *Life with Lloyd George*, edited by Colin Cross, Macmillan, 1975, pp. 267–8

† George Cornwallis-West (1874–1951) had married, in 1900, Lady Randolph Churchill, mother of Winston, who was some twenty years his senior. The marriage was dissolved in 1913 and he then married the actress Mrs Patrick Campbell.

a long lease to the Duke of Westminster. The latter found it a convenient addition to his shoots at World's End and Palé, and it was of course easily accessible from Eaton Hall.

In 1921, for reasons I have never discovered, the Duke gave up his lease and the Cornwallis-Wests decided to sell; Uncle Alfred bought it, lock, stock and barrel. The ten thousand acres included three separate grouse moors and further manorial rights, giving four driving days, but the great fame of Llanarmon has always been the pheasant shoot. In an article in *The Field* during the 1930s on the 'six best stands in Britain', two at Llanarmon were included, Precipice Wood and the Pool. I was to know these stands intimately over the next fifty years.

However, in August 1940 things were on a very restricted basis, though to me, a sixteen-year-old who adored the country and any sport that was going, it seeemed a paradise.

Uncle Alfred and Aunt Ethel had moved up from Marchwiel, their home near Wrexham, to spend the late summer at Llanarmon, living in The Towers, a gothic-style shooting lodge built by the Duke, with no electricity of course and basic plumbing. Nevertheless, Uncle Alfred's butler, Cousins, and John the footman had come too, the headkeeper's wife, Mrs Beaton, cooked, and for wartime we seemed to live very well. I slept in one of the seemingly endless row of 'bachelor' bedrooms in a tin-roofed annexe that had been added at the rear.

Uncle Alfred lent me a twenty-bore, made by Henry Monk of Chester, and I spent my days going out under the eye of Beaton or Edwards, the second keeper. Beaton was a Scot, married to a Welsh wife, while Llew Edwards was a local; they had served together in Mesopotamia in the First War and had many good tales to tell. Two other younger keepers had joined up, leaving one other much older man called Tom, who only seemed to appear occasionally.

We rarely came back without a heavy bag, generally of rabbits and pigeons, though I can distinctly remember my first snipe.

Then came the first day at the grouse, on the home moor. Uncle Alfred was about sixty and most of his guests, including Tom Butler-Lloyd, Captain Hutchinson, Sir Archibald Nye and others, were, I suppose, his contemporaries, so I was vastly privileged to be taking part and had been given strict instructions by the keepers. I was put at the end of the line, and in the second drive, got my first grouse – I can see it fall now! I was hooked, and have remained so.

In these days it seems amazing that we managed without anything mechanised at all; Uncle Alfred rode a pony, but everyone else walked everywhere and somehow the lunch-hut was laid out when we got there. Several more wonderful days followed, in perfect weather, and soon we were into September. We walked up partridges, in a little valley called Dolwen where there is a fifteenth-century house that has associations with Owen Glendower, and I shot my first partridge.

Then we made an expedition to Pentre Foelas, beyond Corwen, on the old A5 where Uncle Alfred had for some time leased the shooting at a place called Gile. Here we stayed for two nights in the Saracen's Head, at Cerrig-y-Druidion, and shot all manner of things. There was a very good snipe bog, plenty of partridges and even a small grouse moor. My cousin Jimmie was with us; he had recently left his first wife, Peggy, and was accompanied by Mary Read, who was to be wife number two and whom I thought the most lovely creature I had ever seen. There were also two very pretty Welsh maids in the hotel, with whom we sat up late into the night singing songs until Uncle Alfred sent down word to tell us to shut up and go to bed.

Captain Hutchinson, known to all as 'Hutch', was a regular guest at Llanarmon and a considerable character. His stories were always of an indelicate nature but told with such panache that he got away with it; he was a particular favourite with my Aunt Ethel. His great claim to fame was to have invented Blue Cheshire cheese, entirely by accident. The Cheshire cheese company, for whom he worked, one day threw out a batch of cheeses that had 'gone wrong'. Hutch examined one, asked the foreman how they had come to that condition and promptly marketed them independently. For a man who had no shooting of his own he seemed to enjoy a wide list of invitations; once, after shooting with the then Lord Bicester, he accompanied his thank-you letter with one of his cheeses. His lordship's pleasure was rather dented when, a few days later, he received a bill.

Another guest that summer for the grouse shooting was the General

Llanarmon, November 1963 – left the author, behind Nick Cayzer, back to camera Justin MacKeurtan, centre headkeeper Alf Matthews confers with Jimmie McAlpine, behind them Jack Bissill, right Donny Stevens and Jack Brittain-Jones

Officer commanding Western Command, whose name now escapes me but whose major contribution to the day's sport was that he produced a platoon of soldiers who performed as beaters.

Although my weeks that summer at Llanarmon were, in retrospect, idyllic and, thanks to the generosity of Uncle Alfred, made me a shooting addict for life, the war was never very far away. Frequently, we would watch in the evening, from the front door of The Towers, as wave after wave of German bombers passed overhead on their way to bomb Birkenhead and Liverpool. They had flown from French airfields and came up the Irish Sea and thus in from the west to avoid our anti-aircraft guns. Several local places were lit up as decoys, including Ruabon mountain, which was bombed night after night and the heather and peat burned for six weeks.

Uncle Alfred had formed his own separate company, Sir Alfred

McAlpine & Son several years earlier, the given reason being that the original firm had become too large and unwieldy and he wished to have a separate entity in Wales and the north-west of England. The true story was that Jimmie, having been sent down from Cambridge in 1927 after one term, joined the family firm in 1928, working as a timekeeper on the contract to build the Firestone Factory on the Great West Road, supervised by his cousin Robin. He told me many years later that his wages were four pounds a week but that it frequently cost him six pounds weekly to balance the time-sheets, so shaky was his arithmetic. Over the next decade he worked on various other contracts but the lights of London proved very tempting and he often had only just returned from the latest nightclub when it was time to start work.

Eventually, in 1935, the uncles, Willy and Malcolm, squared up to their brother Alfred and said they didn't think that Jimmie was going to make the grade. To which Alfred replied, to his credit, that if they felt that way he would take his share of the business out and set up on his own with his son, which he did with lasting success for all concerned.

I must have made a reasonably good impression on my uncle during this long visit, for it was during that time that he suggested to my mother I should come and work for him when I left school. This was to be sooner than I expected.

By mid-September the Battle of Britain was at its height and there seemed every possibility that we were about to be invaded. My mother took the unusual step of informing Mr Cutcliffe that she saw no point in my returning to school on the prescribed date; while delighted to get additional holiday, I soon discovered that most of my friends had gone back and managed to persuade my anxious parent that Northampton-shire was as safe as Surrey.

By now I had moved on to the science side of the school, which meant that I spent at least one week each term in one of the several workshops which I have already described. That autumn I spent a busy week in the metal-working shop, finishing off breech blocks for 4.5 anti-aircraft guns, and felt I was at last doing something useful in the war. At the same time I started getting interested in explosives. It was very easy to obtain the necessary ingredients from the chemistry labs, and some of us had some exciting afternoons blowing small holes in a farmer's field a mile from Grafton, without damaging ourselves.

During the Christmas holidays I alternated between Owlswood and my father's flat in Chiltern Court, where we had to spend most nights in the air-raid shelter; Baker Street Station received a direct hit one night, which was uncomfortably close. By daylight the streets were a sorry sight, gaping holes in buildings, a tangle of firemen's hoses and glass and rubble everywhere. June, by then, had a vitally important job looking after the welfare of the many thousands who slept nightly in rows on the underground stations, organising tea and other necessaries; she worked like a Trojan.

At Churt, an enormous shelter had been created, sixty feet below ground, with several separate rooms, including an elaborate bedroom for Taid, with telephone. He had become very jittery about bombs (nineteen landed on the farm during the war, not, I am sure, intended for him, but for Aldershot; the Germans mistook the lake below Bron y de for the Little Pond at Frensham, which had been deliberately drained) and spent every night in this very expensive dug-out. David and I slept there one night and tried some of Taid's Irish whiskey – not a success.

Nain was at Criccieth, having slipped on a parquet floor a month before, at her sister-in-law's house, and cracked a hip. This was to have fatal consequences.

On 12 December, Lord Lothian, our Ambassador to the United States, died suddenly. As Philip Kerr he had been a private secretary to LG from 1916–21; he became the 11th Marquess in 1930. He had only been in Washington for a year, and his death was a considerable shock to Taid who had lunched with him just a month previously. Churchill tried to persuade LG to go as the new ambassador, but he pleaded his age (he was about to be seventy-eight) and got Lord Dawson to write a letter confirming that he was physically not up to it. This was the last attempt that was made to get him actively involved in the war effort.

I spent New Year with Uncle Gwilym, Aunt Edna, David and William at Tenby, in their house in Hayward's Lane, where I recall great celebrations at news of the capture of Bardia. Milford Haven docks had been severely bombed and were still burning while I was there, a great pall of smoke hanging in the sky. Then I moved on to Bristol to stay a few nights with Valerie and Goronwy in their first home, a flat in Clifton. Goronwy had become a lecturer in the university and Valerie was also teaching; the bombing there had been very bad for several weeks.

I had been back at Oundle barely a week when Nain died, at Criccieth. Following her fall six weeks before she developed pneumonia and went downhill rapidly. As soon as Taid was warned how serious matters were, he arranged first for a specialist to go from Liverpool, then for Lord Dawson, accompanied by AJ, to travel to Criccieth from London, while he himself set out from Churt. The weather was atrocious and at Cerrig-y-Druidion the snow made it impossible to move any farther; at one point the Rolls, with George Dyer at the wheel, was completely buried. AJ persuaded the GWR to lay on a special train from Corwen but the snowplough preceding it ran off the rails and in spite of the efforts of gangs of men working in the dark it was hopeless. LG was utterly stranded in the White Lion at Cerrig-y-Druidion, while his beloved Maggie lay dying sixty miles away.

I only learnt all these tragic details much later from my father, who had been very concerned that the shock, and subsequent strain of the funeral, might be fatal for Taid. Countless messages of sympathy poured into Brynawalon, from the King and Queen, Roosevelt, Smuts and many lesser known notables. But the one he treasured most came from 10 Downing Street:

My dear David,

I learned with great sorrow of the death of your wife – that great woman, who embodied all that is most strong and true in the British race. I offer you my deep sympathy in the severance of a wonderful tie that has lasted through the storms and vicissitudes of two generations. But, pray, believe me, how much Clemmie and I feel for you and your children in their sad hour.

Yours always,

W.*

* Churchill was the only one of LG's political friends who called him 'David'.

As ever, AJ had been a tower of strength during these testing days. In his diary he recorded, 'From the time of Dame Margaret's death, LG's health steadily degenerated.'

In a conversation that I had with him the following year, I noted him as saying, 'It is my firm belief that he has not yet completely got over your grandmother's death. She meant more to him than even he realised before.' I believe this to be true.

I had now passed School Certificate, at the second attempt, and, if the reader can believe it, actually got 'very good' in English. This was to be the only examination I ever did pass. As my father pointed out, even if I succeeded in getting into Cambridge I should inevitably be in the army before long, and it would probably be much better if I left school now and took up Uncle Alfred's offer to join McAlpine's. This idea certainly appealed to me, as I felt I would be doing something useful in the war, and thus, after long talks with Cutcliffe and Bud Fisher, my schooldays were rapidly numbered. I actually left Oundle a month before my seventeenth birthday.

CHAPTER 6

My First Job

Corsham is one of the most charming of Wiltshire villages, with its row of Flemish weavers' houses, its seventeenth-century almshouses and Corsham Court, the seat of the Methuen family for many generations. But in 1941 it was called upon to play an unlikely role.

For several hundred years the Bath and Portland Stone Company had been operating its quarries in the area, cutting out the oolite stone, rich cream in colour, which lies in a seam roughly twelve feet in thickness and at a depth of about a hundred feet. Before the war the War Office had taken over a considerable area of worked-out quarry for the storage of ammunition; just inside the Corsham portal of Box Tunnel a well-guarded branch line led into this underground arsenal.

Now a far larger and more ambitious project was under way: the installation of no fewer than three of the major armaments manufacturers' works in this vast natural air-raid shelter; for the task Sir Alfred McAlpine & Son had been appointed main contractor. Here I arrived on 26 May to start work; I recall a very hot and long walk from Corsham station to the site, which extended over a huge area. Alistair Kennedy was the site agent and took me under his wing, arranging for me to be a lodger in the same house as himself, with a pleasant, middle-aged couple called Truelove.

Pickwick House is an elegant, small Georgian house in Bath stone, on the London road, with an attractive garden. Mr Truelove was a civil servant, had spent many years in Nigeria and was the resident engineer for the War Office installation I have described above. He and his wife were both very kind to me during my stay and made me feel immediately at home.

For those unfamiliar with the world of contracting, a word of explanation may be helpful. The contractor is generally selected on a competitive basis from a shortlist and signs a contract to carry out the job for a fixed sum on behalf of the client – who may be a private individual, a large public company or a government department. The client will appoint an architect to supervise the works and see that the contractor carries out the works correctly; in the case of a civil engineering contract there will be, instead of an architect, a firm of consulting engineers, who will have been responsible for the design of the project in the first place.

At Corsham, which was a very large contract of great complexity, the client was the Ministry of Aircraft Production and the consulting engineers were the leading firm of Sir Alexander Gibb & Partners, who had a substantial resident staff on site. McAlpine contracts were normally conducted by a resident agent (a qualified civil engineer) working in tandem with a works manager, an unqualified but highly experienced man who had risen 'through the ranks' and whose concern was the employment of labour and the mechanical side of carrying out the job.

Such was the complexity of Corsham that Alistair Kennedy, as agent, also had the unusual additional presence of a chief executive. The latter was in the formidable form of Bob McGregor, a director of the company, who, together with Mr Shaw, had followed Uncle Alfred when he broke away from his brothers and created his own company in 1935. Bob was an alarming Highlander, with flashing eyes and an uncertain temper but with the driving determination to get things done that had fuelled him for the past forty years. Under Alistair Kennedy was a chief engineer (John Evans, succeeded later by Roderick David) and a considerable team of talented junior engineers, many of whom later became stars in the McAlpine firmament, such as Stewart McVey and Bob Cousins. There was also a small, rotund Welshman called Les Howells, whose responsibilities were now widened to include knocking me into shape and inducting me into to the mysteries of civil engineering.

Initially these revolved round the use of theodolite and level, which, together with a set of ranging rods, were the main tools with which an engineer in those days (and I imagine now) set out his work, whether it was a building, a main sewer or a tunnel. For the first few weeks I helped Wilf Jones, Les Howell's chainman, to lug the equipment around the site, holding the staff, which was marked in feet and inches, and generally learning what was involved. With a reasonable level of maths in my head from Oundle and a certain aptitude for that sort of thing, I quite quickly became sufficiently skilled to be entrusted with tasks on my own.

Over the three hundred years that the Bath and Portland Stone Company had been extracting their valuable material from underground, they had adhered to a simple method of leaving natural columns of stone every few yards to support the roof. This had not been done to any particular pattern, however, so that a plan of the quarry showing these quite large pillars looked like an enormous and complicated jigsaw puzzle. Fitting in working areas for the manufacture of aircraft engines was to prove full of problems. But initially there was a more urgent task; over the years the quarrymen had encountered layers of unsuitable stone, known as 'brash', which they carefully stacked behind them as they extracted the more valuable blocks of oolite which were then hauled to the surface, dressed and trundled down the road to build those immaculate terraces in Bath and Bristol.

There were about four million cubic yards of this 'brash' to be removed before any installations could be made and the only way of removing it was via several existing vertical shafts, using a crane and skip, a slow and laborious method. A slope shaft was therefore dug, a conveyor-belt laid, and the stone discharged at ground level into trucks running on a makeshift railway line. This line rapidly extended out into the adjoining farmland as the 'Yankee' wagons, as they were called, pulled by steam locomotives, tipped their loads. One of my early efforts was to set out an extension of this line, on a curve, with a large gang of Irish navvies under one Bill Alexander; they followed my line of pegs with sleepers and steel, the whole thing being urged forward by the sparkling presence of Bob McGregor. It was a scene reminiscent of the early days of the Canadian Pacific Railway.

Below ground it was permanently cloudy with dust as the stone was removed by mechanical diggers, lit only by acetylene lamps that gave off an acrid smell. It was very easy to get lost, since one quarry led into another. On one occasion, two of us blundered into the adjoining War Office territory, where were stored many millions of rounds of ammunition; we retreated rapidly without being discovered. At another time, I was in a quiet part of the workings when I felt the ground below me tremble and there was a long rumbling sound. It was some time before I realised that I was standing only a few yards above Box Tunnel and an express was passing through.

Returning to ground level in a wooden skip was an exhilarating experience; one was hauled, by a crane situated on the surface, a hundred feet or more up a centuries-old shaft lined with stone, bumping against the clammy walls during the ascent.

There was an immense amount of building going on at ground level as well: vast hostel blocks designed to house the several thousand labourers, mostly Irish, who were initially brought in daily by buses from Bath and Bristol, air-raid shelters, permanent offices and an intricate pattern of access roads to service the whole extraordinary project.

I bicycled great distances that first summer at Corsham, to Bath most often; going there was easy, as it was largely downhill, but the return (about ten miles) up Box Hill was a sweat. One Sunday I did the forty miles to Cheddar by lunchtime, explored Gough's caves and climbed above the cliffs overlooking the gorge. I was back in Pickwick House just before 9 p.m. to listen to Churchill on the wireless; it was 22 June and Hitler had attacked Russia that morning.

Unbelievably, I find from a diary which I kept intermittently at the time that I played cricket for Corsham that summer, which must indicate how desperate they were for players; I have little recollection of the matches, but remember evenings in the Methuen Arms afterwards. There were pleasant afternoons swimming in various rivers, at Beanacre and Slaughterford, with sessions in local pubs later, but I seemed, on the whole, to lead a fairly innocent life. In point of fact I was far too hard up to indulge in riotous living; I see from this same diary that I was paid £2 18s.7d. per week, out of which £2 5s.0d. went towards my lodgings.

Lunch at the site canteen was 1/6*d*. I could earn extra by working on Sundays, and frequently did so, but frugality was the order of the day.

I became very fond of Bath, and have remained so. Those elegant crescents and terraces, the parks and the Abbey had a magical appeal. On sunny afternoons there would be a band playing in Pulteney Gardens, boats on the Avon just below the bridge and children playing happily; the war at such times seemed impossibly remote.

Returning by train late at night, after the pubs had shut, was a different story. Hundreds of very drunken Irishmen would be on the platform singing, fighting or vomiting; quite often the train's arrival would be delayed after one particularly inebriated soul had fallen on to the track and had had to be rescued by his mates. It was important to pick one's compartment with care, as a thirty-minute journey with such companions could be full of hazards. But I do not wish to disparage these Irish workers; they had been loyal to McAlpine's for a great many years and went from contract to contract, generally in the same gangs: their output was prodigious and their humour infectious. I made a lot of friends among them when they were sober.

I had not been many months at Corsham before I witnessed a serious accident. The shafts that I have mentioned were used not only for hauling up the 'brash' but for lowering materials. I was working with a theodolite near one where bricks were daily lowered in skips; four men had just filled one skip and were attaching the chains at the corners when the jib of their crane touched an overhead 11,000-volt cable. There was an almighty crack and a blue flash, followed by screams and oaths. Two of the men were killed outright and the other two succumbed within minutes. This was my first experience of sudden death.

Alistair Kennedy had been with the firm for several years, having worked on the Dolgarrog Dam in 1928, but was still only thirty-two when he was appointed agent at Corsham, responsibile for what was then the firm's most prestigious contract and one that had to be completed as rapidly as possible. He was therefore under intense pressure and worked very long hours; nevertheless, he always seemed to find time, whenever we met in the evenings at Pickwick House, however late, to help me master some technicality or put me right in some way. He had a great capacity for absorbing every detail of a subject; if there was any particular fact that he wished to be doubly sure of, it went down on the back of a cigarette packet. He was (and still is) a keen golfer and I frequently caddied for him on the course near Box; these occasions tailed off markedly after he met his wife-to-be, then a Wren on one of the local Admiralty bases. In later years he took over as managing director of the firm, and guided it through a period of rapid expansion in post-war years.

The Trueloves had some domestic rearrangements in July which meant I had to move elsewhere; I was lucky enough to find myself billeted with a charming family called Finch-Noyes, who lived in the Warden's House, just opposite the gates to Corsham Court. This house, as its name implies, was originally lived in by the warden (as in Trollope) who had in his charge the elderly residents of the adjoining almshouses. It was a fascinating building, constructed of stone in the sixteenth century, L-shaped and with an elaborate two-storey porch above the front door. The hall had a gallery at one end, from which, in the eighteenth century, a servant girl had thrown herself to her death and ever after was supposed to haunt the place. Certainly there were dark stains on the floorboards which my hosts assured me could never be removed, but I can't say that I ever saw a ghost. Mr Finch-Noyes was a retired bank manager, and I suspect his career had been a very successful one, since he had a restless, enquiring nature, verging on the fidgety, accompanied by an impish, almost anarchic sense of humour. I found him most engaging and we became good friends. One of his hobbies was wood-turning, which he carried on in a small shed in the garden, smoking furiously all the time.

The Finch-Noyes rented the house from Lord Methuen, with whom they were on very good terms, and as a result I found myself invited to Corsham Court on several occasions, for lunch and so forth. Paul Methuen was of course a gifted artist, had been an RA for many years and was a man of considerable charm.

I have to say that his younger brother Anthony, who lived near by in Ivy House, was a different sort altogether. I had joined the local Home

Guard (once you were seventeen you were eligible) and the Hon. Anthony was our local commanding officer. If he could find any fault he would do so, and was often, I thought, unnecessarily harsh. It didn't bother me much, since having been in the school corps I knew the rudiments of soldiering and could at least handle a rifle, but some of the local boys from the farms were totally out of their depth and received a fearful chastisement. We didn't have enough rifles to go round I recall and when we at last received a bren gun, the Hon. Anthony would not allow us to strip it down as he considered we were far too stupid to ever put it together again. We would parade in the stables at Corsham Court, and plod round the park, pretending to look for Germans. It was all truly *Dad's Army* stuff.

Uncle Alfred visited the site fairly regularly but I hardly got more than a glimpse of him, or a brief enquiry as to how I was getting on. It was implicit that I had my chance and it was up to me to make the most of it. But in September I had a week's leave and found myself once more at Llanarmon pursuing the grouse.

I remember the winter of 1941–2 as being very cold and unpleasant. I had moved back to Pickwick House in the autumn and my room was at the very top of that very cold house; on many occasions my boots, covered in ice and frozen snow from the site, were in the same condition the following morning. It was also, looking back, the time of the war when morale was at its lowest and food rationing was really biting. The mood of exhilaration in 1940, when we had our backs to the wall and had defeated the Luftwaffe, was in the past, and the disasters of Singapore and elsewhere were dampening, to say the least. I occasionally went up to London for a night to see my father, who had been in and out of hospital several times, and the bombing there continued unabated, as elsewhere. Uncle David was also now in London, having been transferred to the Judge Advocate General's department, which was to be his future for the remainder of the war, prosecuting his brother officers.

Underground, the contract started to take shape; most of the waste stone had been removed by early 1942, new lifts were installed for the hoisting of heavy machinery, an elaborate ducting system for ventilation was under way, and the first machines for turning out aircraft engines (for the Bristol Aircraft Company) were in place. I had become a reasonably proficient, if totally unqualified, engineer and was allowed to set out various jobs, but always under the eagle eye of Les Howells. I had started a correspondence course with the Institute of Civil Engineers, with the object of attaining at least the first stage of a qualification, but it never came to anything.

I happened to go home to Haslemere for the weekend of 24–5 April and so missed the bombing of Bath. As is well known, it was one of the so-called *Baedeker* raids, a reprisal for our bombing of Lübeck and other German towns, and there were no defences there at all. The destruction and loss of life (over four hundred) was appalling. McAlpine's mobilised a huge fleet of lorries which, together with several hundred men and digging machines, were engaged for a week helping to dig out casualties and restore some normality to the shattered city.

Later that year, A. J. Sylvester took to spending occasional weekends with friends near Lacock and he and his wife had me to dinner several times there at the Angel. I had not seen him for a year or so and, as always, we picked up where we had left off. One evening we had had a fascinating talk as we always did, and I made some notes afterwards. It was not all that many years since AJ had been very active interviewing leading figures for LG's memoirs, and his recollections of some of them were very fresh in his mind. He thought Clemenceau and LG were the two most forceful men he had ever known; but Clemenceau was vindictive and he gave an example that he had witnessed at a conference during the war. Clemenceau suddenly pointed at an army officer present whom he disliked and asked if he had permission to be present. The answer came, 'No.' 'Well, get out and go to the front!' and the poor devil went.

AJ had unbounded admiration for Smuts. During the First War, LG offered him a position in his cabinet, which Smuts accepted on condition that there would be no home duties. Very soon LG sent him to South Wales to try to settle a miners' strike. Smuts protested that he knew nothing about mining but was told to go just the same. He arrived to find tens of thousands of teeming, angry miners whom he had to address. 'Men,' he said, 'I know nothing about mining, but wherever I have been in our great Empire I have been made aware of the great Welsh reputation for singing – will you please sing for me?'

Of course they began to sing; he said no more, and returned to Downing Street where he received warm congratulations on having settled a tricky and damaging dispute. He protested his bewilderment and told LG, 'You have done this.'

Smuts was the only one of those whom AJ interviewed who asked to see his written-up notes; he corrected just three words, one of which was 'nigger' in a South African context.

AJ gave me the latest news of Taid, who was clearly withdrawing more and more from public life, becoming increasingly pessimistic about the war and still refusing to join Churchill. AJ said Taid did not want to be head of some department under the PM; he wished to be a member of the cabinet, able to express his opinions freely and, above all, to have power. This seemed at odds with his apparent general decline.

In later years, AJ was to make his permanent home near Corsham, where he acquired a farm after the war, became a JP, a keen rider and champion ballroom dancer, and failed by only three weeks to reach his century.

Shortly after my eighteenth birthday I volunteered for the army. My father, who had joined the Royal Engineers in the First War, was keen that I should do the same and, with my new practical experience of civil engineering, it seemed a sensible step; so, when enlisting, I expressed a preference for that corps. I left Corsham towards the end of the year; the contract was completed in 1943 but by that time we had gained air superiority over Germany and the necessity of producing aircraft engines underground had passed. This enormous effort and expenditure was largely wasted; I believe Hawthorn, as the site was named, became, after the war, a vast storage depot for food supplies in the event of a Russian nuclear attack.

I had enjoyed my eighteen months at Corsham, and though it had meant missing that last year at Oundle, I had matured in a different, and certainly more rigorous climate. Now I was about to become a soldier.

CHAPTER 7

Into the Army

I must have received my marching orders by Christmas 1942 because on 7 January following I was on my way to Clitheroe, to join the Royal Engineers Training Battalion there. This was situated in Lower Mill, on the banks of the River Ribble, and a pretty comfortless place it was too. I do not know when it had ceased to be a working mill but the minimum of conversion had been carried out for the sappers' benefit. It was a gaunt, prison-like building of many storeys, in which we slept by companies, one to each floor, in triple-deck wooden bunks on straw palliases, changed infrequently. Drill parades and PT took place in the weaving shed, a vast area on the ground floor, which echoed to the barked commands of sergeants and sergeant-majors.

I joined a platoon of motley characters, all new recruits, whose faces gaze out at me now from a photograph but whose names I have largely forgotten. Robin Lindsay, who had been at Marlborough and remembered me from boxing days, became a good friend but we lost touch when I was transferred. Our platoon sergeant I recall as a friendly soul, an ex-keeper, who helped us to settle in, but his number two, a Corporal Starkey, was an aggressive little man, as was the company commander, Captain Keogh, with whom I had a few altercations during the coming weeks.

Most of our training was carried out on a large field which stretched between Lower Mill and the river. Some days were devoted to what would appear to be World War I routines, unrolling endless coils of barbed wire and fastening same with picket posts, or digging elaborate trenches, revetted with posts and wire netting, and creating a fire step – real trench-warfare stuff. However, we soon progressed to more interesting, if hazardous, exercises, involving the study of the relative merits of various explosives – gun-cotton, ammonal, nitro-glycerine, etc. – together with their fuses and detonators. We handled both our own mines and the Germans', and spent long hours in setting booby traps and dismantling them.

Getting on familiar terms with the intricacies of Bailey-bridge building took up a lot of time; we assembled sections on dry land, dismantled them, put them together again, and repeated the process until each component was as familiar as one's own fingers – after all, it might sometimes be necessary for us to do this in darkness. The day came at last when we assembled a complete bridge and pushed it out across the Ribble, with a long counter-balance so that it reached the far bank without toppling in. We also made pontoon bridges, which, with a strong current then running down from the hills, involved quite a struggle and occasioned a great deal of furious shouting from our instructors.

Clitheroe was like many Lancashire mill towns and not therefore very exciting, though the locals were kindness itself, as I have always found Lancashire folk to be, and full of fun. Apart from the local cinema, various fish and chip shops and the pubs, there was not a lot to do in the town. The surrounding countryside was a different matter. To the east of Clitheroe lay Pendle Hill, a fine stretch of moorland with a pretty village at its foot called Downham, and to the north, over the Ribble, was Waddington from which a road ran up to some hills. Halfway up was the Moorcock where we occasionally treated ourselves to a better than average meal.

I spent ten days in a Nissen hut with two or three others suffering from mumps; for a boy aged eighteen, this could have been a problem, but I was lucky and escaped unscathed. Otherwise we were kept very fit by long hours of training, PT and lengthy route marches over the aforesaid hills, sometimes sleeping out in the rain and wet, finding shelter as best we could. Food was adequate, augmented by whatever the NAAFI could offer, which included very weak beer, dosed (we firmly believed) with bromide to subdue lustful thoughts, though the temptations in Clitheroe were pretty limited. I boxed in one tournament and knocked my man out.

My memory is very hazy as to the exact sequence of events, but, sometime in May or June, I and several others aspiring to be officers found ourselves sent to a War Office selection board at Wrotham. I must have had some leave at about the same time as I remember discussing with Uncle David the length of time it appeared to be going to take before I would have completed my training and my anxiety to go on active service as soon as possible. The upshot was that Uncle David had a word with Sir Terence Nugent, then Brigade Major of London District, and I was instructed to present myself at the regimental headquarters of the Welsh Guards. This was then situated in No.16 Wilton Crescent, an elegant house which I was to get to know in peacetime, after it had been returned to its owners, Wilfred and Nora Janson. I was duly marched into the orderly room where I faced a formidable trio in the form of the regimental lieutenant-colonel, Colonel A. M. Bankier, DSO, MC, Major the Earl of Lisburne, regimental-adjutant, and Major C. H. Dudley-Ward, assistant regimental-adjutant. These three distinguished guardsmen gazed with some astonishment at their visitor, as I was wearing sapper insignia on my rather scruffy forage cap, had a single lance-corporal's stripe on my sleeve (I had been promoted at Clitheroe) and probably saluted with unguardsmanlike precision.

As it so happened I could claim some tenuous connection with the regiment in that my grandfather had played a significant role in the raising of the Welsh Guards in February 1915, in spite of opposition from Kitchener. (Many years later I came across a letter in which he had strongly recommended that the 'flash' on our bearskins should be green and white, being, as he said, the Tudor colours: I duly gave this letter to RHQ.) In any event, David Lloyd George's grandson was now there in the orderly room as an item of curiosity.

Nothing so untoward as described in Evelyn Waugh's *Put Out More Flags* befell me. 'Bertie' Bankier was very kind and I can only recall one question, which was whether I had any private income. As it happened I had: a hundred pounds per annum kindly given me by Uncle Malcolm (McAlpine), who very generously made a similar allowance to every member of the family, whether they were in his firm or not, who had joined up for the duration of the war.

Once I had been accepted for the Welsh Guards things moved remarkably quickly and I never returned to Clitheroe, I was told to report to Pirbright and join the pre-OCTU training course. I was fortunate enough in this as I avoided the dreaded initiation period at Caterham, the Guards' depot, my six months' service presumably having counted for something. My main recollection of the two-month stint at Pirbright is of constant chivvying from alarming Scotsmen – not surprising, for we were under instruction from the Right Flank Company of the Scots Guards Training Battalion. But their bark was on the whole worse than their bite.

We were nearly all about the same age, public-school boys, with a preponderance of Etonians. Dick Berridge was the only contemporary from Oundle that I found; he was killed a year later, in Normandy with the Scots Guards. Some of the officers seemed little older than we were, Simon Bland and Edward Trafford for example.

Training was exhaustive and varied. Long hours on the square (needless to say), weapon training, assault courses, night exercises and learning to drive – the last was one of the real bonuses, as we were instructed in every size and type of vehicle by skilled NCOs, at his majesty's expense too. I had early on tried driving on the farm at West Hill, on a tractor, but a fifteen-hundredweight or three-ton truck on a public road was a different matter, though just as enjoyable. Learning how the things worked was more difficult, though it was child's play compared with a present-day car, which requires a computer to put anything right. Riding a motor bicycle was not something I ever took to with great relish, though we all had to do it; on one occasion I forgot how to stop, accelerated instead, and shot up the steps of the NAAFI, collapsing under my machine at the top – much to the amusement of the girls cooking lunch.

The course was soon over and after a short spell of leave it was on to the next stage, four months at 161st (RMC) OCTU at Mons Barracks, Aldershot. I was in C Company, commanded by John Chandos-Pole, and more immediately, No. 15 Platoon, commanded by Captain the Viscount Vaughan. John, who, was soon to succeed his father as Earl of Lisburne, has now been a friend for fifty years and we are neighbours in

Wales. He has the most delightful sense of humour, and at Mons, while insisting that we did what was required of us, made it abundantly clear that he could not regard soldiering as something to be taken too seriously. We all loved him for this and consequently (I hope) never let him down. Additionally, we were particularly proud of our platoon officer, since he was the only one to wear a medal ribbon, gained, as he told me years later, for services rendered at the Coronation in 1937, 'dealing with tricky peeresses'.

There were eight of us cadets who were potential Welsh Guards officers, a similar number destined for the Irish Guards and others joining various infantry regiments of the line. Because we had been accepted as officer material, the training was very intense and fairly demanding both on body and mind, with long hours at drill and physical training, interspersed with lectures on every conceivable subject from military law to venereal disease. The hours on the parade ground were made especially alarming by the presence of RSM 'Tibby' Brittain, Coldstream Guards, a man with an incredible word of command and the highest standards of drill. Woe betide any cadet who appeared with dirty equipment, or who moved one hundredth of a second after the others; 'fourth man in the back row – take his name Sergeant Dyer!' On a foggy morning, of which there were plenty at Aldershot, it was frequently impossible for Brittain actually to see the marching columns, but when he gave the command to halt they were exactly where he wanted them.

I managed to get over to Haslemere quite often at weekends, and took a friend sometimes. Robin O'Kelly was a particular chum and shared my love of shooting; there was one little valley on Blackdown that always held woodcock and we had some happy afternoons pursuing them. Robin promised to take me to shoot at his home in Ireland when the war was over, but he was killed the following year in France.

On one of these weekends at home I recall Uncle David getting back late in the evening, flinging the *Evening Standard* down and saying, 'Well, your Taid has made an honest woman of her at last!' A picture on the front page showed him with Frances Stevenson, after their registry office wedding in Guildford that afternoon. It may sound incredible now but I had to ask my stepfather what he meant; I was so naïve that even at the age of nineteen I had not realised that this affair had been going on for thirty years. Taid was then eighty and Frances I suppose in her early fifties; the marriage was bitterly opposed by his children, especially Megan who refused to speak to him. I went over to Churt a couple of times that autumn and found a big difference; he had aged dramatically in the past two years and lost a lot of his fire.

About the middle of December we were dispatched for a fortnight to Capel Curig, where an arduous battle school had been devised as a sort of *bombe surprise* at the end of our cadet training. We were billeted in the stables of the Royal Goat Hotel and during the day clambered about the foothills of Snowdonia, firing live ammunition and hurling grenades in increasingly vile weather. We were usually too exhausted by dark to do much, but I remember walking with Keith Jones one evening to Cobden's Hotel, at the other end of the village. Captain Cobden was then still very much alive and in charge and had the reputation of turning away anyone who displeased him. We must have made a favourable impression since he gave us a very good dinner and we drank a great deal.

These two weeks ended in disaster. The final exercise consisted of us being dropped out of a three-tonner, in pairs, all over the countryside, with a map reference to reach within a certain number of hours, and under strict orders not to use any public roads or railways. The weather was truly atrocious by now, lashing rain alternating with snow and all the rivers swollen. Two of our companions, Dick Swain and Brian Gimson, must have tried to cross the River Conway somewhere near Llanrwst and got swept away, neither being strong swimmers even in normal conditions, let alone wearing battledress and equipment. When they failed to report in, frantic searches were made all night, but to no avail – it was obvious that they were gone. We returned to the south, somewhat downcast, went on leave for Christmas, and returned to Mons for our passing out.

Before the ceremony, the embryo officer had to be translated from his cocoon by a series of visits to expensive West End tailors and haberdashers. Johns and Pegg, of Clifford Street, were the Welsh Guards' regimental tailors and produced my service dress uniform with its solitary ensign's star on the shoulder. Messrs Cole produced shirts and a visit to Herbert Johnson was required for a gold-braided forage cap, plus the more prosaic service dress cap. We got an allowance for all this but, as Philip Brutton has pointed out in his book,* it only met about half the total; Colonel Bertie Bankier's enquiry about private means was not an idle one.

About our actual passing-out parade, I have only the haziest recollection; I think we had a very wild party in the evening, and the late lamented Torquil Matheson has reminded me more than once that thunder-flashes were in action later on.

Be that as it may, I certainly reported to the training battalion at Sandown Park, Esher, in a very sober and submissive mood. As a newly joined ensign one was a very lowly figure; nevertheless there was a very generous spirit in the battalion and one soon settled in to the life. A racecourse may seem an incongruous place to locate troops but Sandown was adapted to this purpose very easily. The lower areas of the grandstand and tote housed the guardsmen, the weighing-in room became the battalion orderly room, the officers' mess was in the restaurant and the adjutant (Bernard Greer when I arrived) was housed in the royal box. When the war was over and the place was handed back to the racecourse authority I believe total barrack damages were assessed at fifty pounds and a plaque recording this may be seen near the weighing-in room; not a bad record after five years of occupation.

The car park made an excellent parade ground and there was of course the very extensive racecourse itself for every sort of training. With the exception of the adjutant, officers were billeted out with various landladies in Esher; I was in a very pleasant little house just by the railway line near Thames Ditton, very handy for returning late from London; my servant, Guardsman Watts, kept me in good working order and life as a nineteen-year-old ensign really seemed very agreeable.

* *Ensign in Italy*, Leo Cooper, 1992

The commanding officer was Tom Oakshott, who had been with the regiment in 1917–18; not a very exciting person, he nevertheless ran things efficiently. His great passion seemed to be bridge. There were a number of other officers who were survivors from that earlier conflict; Cecil Wigan was one and he was my company commander to begin with, a kindly, laconic individual who made life fun. 'Squiff' Ellis, who had reputedly led his men at Ginchy swinging his walking stick, and had been awarded the DSO and MC, and who subsequently was the author of a first-rate history of the regiment, was another company commander.

Then there were a number of 'older' subalterns who, for a variety of reasons, generally physical or to do with age, had not joined one of the three active battalions. Among these I recall Walter Thursby-Pelham, who before the war had had an enviable life teaching cricket to the sons of an eminent Indian Rajah; Cyril Daniels, who would today be described as a 'confirmed bachelor'; and Jack Clayton, who looked after the battalion transport and was a heavy punter on the turf. Hugh Quennell was an unusual character; a very clever City solicitor, he had a great reputation as a 'fixer' of complicated deals, and in wartime seemed to have unrivalled access to things that were in short supply.

One day the major-general decided to inspect the training battalion. All had gone well and the small but distinguished party of Tom Oakshott, Bernard Greer, the RSM and others were accompanying the great man towards the officers' mess for a pre-prandial glass of sherry. At that moment a three-tonner drove slowly past and stopped at the back door to the mess. More from mild curiosity than anything else the major-general enquired what the vehicle might be conveying. The commanding officer asked the adjutant who asked the regimental sergeant-major who barked at his accompanying drill-sergeant, who in turn sprang upon the unsuspecting driver.

'Wos in your vehicle, 92 Jones?'

Back came the immortal words: 'Mr Quennell's kümmel, sir!'

Charles Lewis was one of the most engaging officers there: a rather Woosterish figure, he drove very fast cars and was a brilliant pianist. Even after a great deal of port he could play by the hour. Several of the older officers were married and had their wives with them in their billets; Jock Roderick was one and Norris Kennard another. Norris was a highly civilised person who had been at the Wallace Collection and also became a great expert on armour; his very glamorous American wife Lee used to drive an open Mercedes wearing a very dashing white leather helmet. She was a direct descendant of George Washington. After Cecil Wigan left to join the Westminster garrison for a spell, my company commander was Tom Cundy, a charming man who in peacetime farmed in Nottinghamshire.

There was a constant coming and going of officers: people going on courses, going on leave, being promoted or being drafted to the 3rd Battalion, at this time the only one of the three battalions to be actively engaged with the enemy, in Italy. Bernard Greer went there in about April, to take over as adjutant, and was succeeded at Sandown by David Llewellyn, one of four brothers, who later became an MP and for many years a racing columnist.

I went over to Churt a few times that spring to see Taid and Frances. It was depressing to see how low he had become; his attitude to the war was strange. On one occasion I recall taking Keith Jones and, I think, Frank Hughes with me. After supper we trooped through to the library, anticipating the nine o'clock news (it was the time of Anzio and Cassino). Not a bit of it; the old man sat down in his usual wing chair, Frances switched on the wireless and we had to listen for fifteen minutes to the appalling Lord Haw-Haw. We all turned him on occasionally as a bad joke, but Taid paid rapt attention to his lies and deceit as if it were gospel; I was acutely embarrassed. It was not until the following year, after his death, that I realised his fatal illness had already taken hold and that the drugs he was taking almost certainly caused his depression and lack of vitality.

The other relative whom I was able to see quite regularly was Uncle Malcolm, who lived only a mile or so away from Esher at Fairmile Court, Cobham. Then in his late sixties, he was as vigorous as ever and had played an important role in the invasion plan, though his only comment to me at the time was to the effect that 'he had been trying to do his bit'. In fact, he had become chairman of the group that built the Mulberry harbour, that amazing construction which was towed across the English Channel and within days formed a vital port for our bridgehead on the French coast. He was also brought in by the War Office to study, as an engineer, aerial photographs of the Pas de Calais; he correctly identified the curious long concrete trenches as the launching ramps for the V1s.

On 6th April, I reported to Wellington Barracks, to join the Westminster garrison, a composite battalion, drawn from all the regiments of the brigade, whose function it was to provide protection at a variety of key points in London, as well as mounting King's Guard. Our half-company (the other half being Irish Guards) was commanded by Paul Makins, the subaltern was Norris Kennard and I was the ensign. We drilled by the hour before we were considered competent enough to mount guard; in those days somewhat low-key in appearance – no colours, steel helmets and battledress – it was still an awesome experience for us when we marched into the forecourt of Buckingham Palace for the first time and faced the old guard whom we were relieving. Unknown to me, my parents had arranged to meet and come to watch me on my first guard mounting; my mother was so overcome that my father had to take her home in a taxi.

Guards were of forty-hour duration, long enough to settle in to the comforts of St James's Palace, where one could entertain ladies to luncheon. Apart from my mother and Uncle David I recall that I once invited Aunt Megan, which turned out to be a near disaster. I had told her to ask for the 'officers' guardroom' but, after leaving her taxi, she told the corporal on duty that she had come to 'see an officer in the guardroom'. As it happened we had, at that time, a Lieutenant-Colonel in, I think, the Royal Army Service Corps, under close arrest for some serious sexual misdemeanour, and it was to this unhappy officer that my aunt was conducted. Apparently they looked speechlessly at each other for some moments before she protested that this was not her darling nephew, and somewhat late and a bit flustered she arrived safely and was revived with a martini. The food and drink on guard was (and I am sure still is) superb; one of the ensign's duties was to do 'rounds' at two in the morning, and many a young officer only managed this by clutching firmly the bayonet scabbard of the sergeant who preceeded him in the dark. I dined as a guest, many years later, with Jerry Spencer-Smith when he was captain of the guard; Willy Pratt, a famous ex-steeplechase jockey, was a fellow guest and at the end of the evening he was so tight that he fell from the top of the stairs to the bottom, but avoided injury by performing some three somersaults on the way, just as if he was at Aintree.

At Wellington Barracks there was an 'inlying platoon', the officer commanding which had also to keep an eye on the Downing Street guard. The picquet officer, whose role also fell to me at regular intervals, had the usual variety of chores to perform, including the closing of the sergeants' mess at 23.00 hours, which invariably involved being given a very stiff drink. I still have my copy of operational orders for the picquet officer, signed by Alan Bristowe, who was adjutant, and it contains the fascinating instruction:

> On receipt of the Code Word 'Garden of Eden' he will refer to the sealed orders, so entitled, kept in Safe 'C' in the Orderly Room, and report forthwith to the Adjutant or Assistant Adjutant.

I long to know, even after fifty years, what desperate measures might have had to be taken if this charming code word had ever been received.

There were some interesting, and colourful, characters to be found in the mess, which was by no means limited in use to members of the battalion but seemed to be used as a haven by numerous courtiers from Buckingham Palace and elsewhere; Tommy Leicester, who was equerry to the King, and Billy Fellowes, the agent at Sandringham, I remember in particular. John Sparrow, later warden of All Souls, was then a captain in the Coldstream, as was Peter Daubeny, who had lost an arm in North Africa and was to have such a successful career in the theatre. It was here that I first met John Grigg, then a Grenadier, who became a very dear friend; as I write this he is about to resume work on his marvellous biography of LG – a self-imposed task which has rightly won him much praise and delighted our family.

In command was Lieutenant-Colonel Lord Edward Hay, Grenadier Guards, a veteran of the 1914–18 War and a splendid looking figure,

who was also immensely kind to young officers and deservedly popular.
I am not sure how it came about, but one day Eddie Hay and another
officer accepted an invitation from a senior member of the London
County Council sanitation department to do a little tour of the sewers.
They descended somewhere near Westminster Bridge and walked along
a main sewer, teeming with large rats, for a considerable distance. As
they eventually paused at a junction, Colonel Eddie pointed to a
smaller tunnel, sloping upwards, and asked where that went. After their
guide had consulted his map by torchlight and confessed he had never
seen it before, they decided to investigate further and followed the
tunnel for a short distance until it ended at an iron grille. Removing this
without too much trouble they were astounded to find themselves in a
vault of the Bank of England! Colonel Eddie's description of this little
jaunt was one of the best things I have ever heard. Sadly he was among
those who lost their lives a few weeks later when the Guards' Chapel
was hit by a V1 during matins. John Grigg has told me that he owed his
survival of that awful event to the fact that he was excused church
parade and was sitting in his room above the mess, reading the Book of
Job, when the device landed, blowing him into the fireplace.

Kenneth Rose, whom I met first at the training battalion and who has
been a firm friend for fifty years, owed his life to the fact that Eddie Hay
unexpectedly gave him weekend leave the day before the catastrophe.
Kenneth went on to serve in the armoured battalion in Normandy.

Tom Ford, another Grenadier, was second-in-command; he had lost
an eye in the earlier conflict and the glass one that replaced it was so ill-
fitting that it was difficult to tell at whom he was actually looking. This
gave rise to an hilarious episode one morning at Commanding Officer's
Memoranda, which Tom was taking in Colonel Eddie's absence. Three
Welsh Guardsmen were marched in on some misdemeanour; after
having heard the details Tom looked up at the first one and said, 'Well,
what have you got to say for yourself?' Second guardsman starts, 'I
thank you, sir, for leave to speak . . . ' Tom (looking at him), 'Shut up, I
wasn't talking to you!' Third guardsman, 'I never said a word, sir.'

I know that Norris and I, standing behind Tom, had great difficulty in
keeping our faces straight.

I kept a very sketchy diary at the time and though the ink is very faded I can just read my writing for an entry in late April, 'Met Michael Bonsor in Piccadilly; he, Shane [Jameson] and I had tea, then to Berkeley, joined Peter [Comyns] and Ted Rider. Got box for Jack Hulbert show – Quaglino's where joined Hugh Griffiths's party – Astor until 2.30.' Thus did a young officer spend an unprofitable evening.

Sometime in May I was back at the training battalion and expecting to get a posting any day to either the 1st Battalion (now in a state of readiness for the invasion) or possibly to the 3rd Battalion. Instead, on 1 June, Keith Jones and I found ourselves on a train to Scotland where we joined 201 Guards Brigade, recently returned from Italy. We were messing with the Irish Guards, who were very friendly, but I really cannot recall why we were sent there. On 6 June, the long-awaited invasion started and within forty-eight hours we received a message from Ernest Lisburne recalling us to Esher for a draft, following embarkation leave. As we were then told to draw tropical kit and get various inoculations it was obvious that our destination was the Mediterranean. We learnt in due course that at Piccolo the 3rd Battalion had had fifteen officer casualties and four of us (Keith, Sam Hall, Frank Hughes and myself) were to be flown out as immediate replacements.

On leave I made a round of farewells, including a visit to Churt, where I saw Taid for the last time. My father had been poorly for some time and was just about to go into Hammersmith Hospital with suspected tuberculosis (the tests proved positive and he lost a lung later in the year).

Drafts leaving the training battalion were normally of some size, officers, NCOs and guardsmen all in one contingent, and would be accompanied by the pipes and drums and seen off with some ceremony by the commanding officer and adjutant. By contrast, our departure was very low key; we four ensigns just got ourselves on a train from Waterloo to Newquay, and at about midnight on 20 June took off in a York bomber from St Mawgan's airfield: active service had at last begun.

CHAPTER 8

With the 3rd Battalion in Italy

I still have a very damp-stained piece of paper on which is typed the following:

> 2/Lt. O. Lloyd George WG is proceeding by air. His journey is of urgent National importance and its deferment to a later stage of the year would be detrimental to the National interest.
>
> signed [indecipherable]
for D. of O.

As the four of us flew out over the Atlantic, each armed with his personalised version of the above, we might have been excused for thinking that the future of the Italian campaign would be in jeopardy until we reached the front line. But as so often was the case with the War Office, the initial urgency of our departure lapsed into a snail-like progress. When we got to Algiers no one seemed particularly interested in us and we were there for nearly a week awaiting transport on, during which time I recall we went to the opera, among other diversions. It was a curious production (which I have never seen performed again) called, according to Keith Jones, *The Three Wise Virgins*. Eventually we managed to join a mixed party of all services in an ancient Dakota and got to Naples, from where we at last reached the Infantry Reinforcement Training Depot at Benevento. This was a few miles east of Caserta, where Supreme Allied Headquarters occupied the old royal palace. While in Naples I recall that, since none of us had any Italian, Keith Jones, being a Balliol scholar, addressed the natives in his best Latin, with remarkable success.

The IRTD was commanded at that time by Harcourt Vernon, with

Willy Lindsay as second-in-command. He seemed amazingly old to us, and was, I suppose, in his middle forties. We found several Welsh Guards officers there: Bill Stephenson, an old hand, who made us very welcome and helped in every way; Mick Grogan I remember, and Johnny Davies, recently returned from the battalion, who cheered us up with lurid details of the 'blood bath' awaiting us further north.

At last we set off, with about twenty non-commissioned officers and guardsmen, by train, which went very slowly and stopped frequently. But it was amazing that a line was working at all, given the total destruction in places like Cassino, which we passed through and saw was an utter shambles. For a totally accurate, and very human, pictorial record of what the Italian battlefront looked like, I can think of nothing better than Edward Seago's *With the Allied Armies in Italy*, which comprises a collection of oils and watercolours which he executed during the second half of 1944, while he was attached to Field Marshal Alexander's headquarters. They are very poignant.

When we eventually reached the 3rd Battalion, in early July, they were out of the line, having a rest after the capture of Perugia, and were based on the shores of Lake Trasimeno. This battalion had come into being in October 1941, had sailed for North Africa in February 1943 and taken a leading part in the Tunisian campaign, adding the names Fondouk and Hammam Lif to the regiment's battle honours. It then moved to the Italian front in February 1944 and held Cerasola above the Garigliano against fierce German attacks and in atrocious weather conditions. Cassino followed, then Arce and Piccolo. It was therefore a seasoned and efficient fighting battalion which with 3rd Grenadier Guards and 2nd Coldstream formed 1st Guards Brigade, part of the 6th Amoured Division. Jocelyn Gurney had assumed command a few weeks previously, with Robin Rose-Price as second-in-command; Francis Egerton was adjutant, having taken over from Bernard Greer a fortnight earlier when the latter walked in his sleep out of a window and broke a leg.

Because of my sapper experience, I was made pioneer officer, my predecessor, Ronnie Furse, having had the misfortune of being injured by one of his own trip-wires, which blinded him in one eye. I was therefore in Support Company, commanded by John de Rutzen; the other officers were Kemmis Buckley, mortars, Hugh Arbuthnot, carrier platoon and Joe Gurney in charge of the anti-tank platoon.

We were a motorised battalion, and Support Company had a plethora of vehicles, mainly bren-gun carriers and jeeps. I had two of these in my platoon as well as a white scout car, which carried our mine-detectors, explosives and miscellaneous stores. My platoon sergeant, Jack Hughes, was aged forty – old enough to be my father (and in fact had a son in the regiment) – and had joined in the late twenties. While in North Africa he had exercised the curious privilege that was extended to the pioneer sergeant of being allowed to grow a beard, and being of a rather saturnine appearance anyway, was now known throughout the battalion as 'Wog' Hughes. He was a native of Bethesda, in North Wales, and a strong supporter of my Aunt Megan, Liberal MP for Anglesey; he would frequently ask, 'Have you heard from your auntie?'

The role of the pioneer platoon was fairly wide-ranging, and as well as detecting and lifting mines or booby traps, included the putting together of any strange contraptions that might be needed, mending bridges (on a small scale) and even producing crosses for those killed. The guardsmen under my command tended therefore to be, in civilian life, artisans such as carpenters or bricklayers, and a very fine lot they were too.

I settled into Support Company very quickly and happily. John de Rutzen, while being a thoroughly professional soldier who demanded the highest standards from his officers and men, had a most engaging personality and a whimsical sense of humour. He was also an accomplished poet, though some of his efforts were distinctly bawdy. His family had lived at Slebech Park, in Pembrokeshire, for many generations and he was a friend of Uncle Gwilym, who was his local member. Having joined the regiment in the early 1930s he would have been, I suppose, about thirty-eight when I joined his company: I can remember Hugh Arbuthnot, aged twenty-one, saying to me (twenty) one day: 'Pretty good, you know, that old bugger being out here at his age.' We all called him Uncle John, and loved him dearly.

Hugh had one great passion in life which was fox-hunting, and he drove his carriers about as if in full cry, often producing a hunting horn for good measure. Shortly after I arrived he received word that his elder brother

Robert had been killed in action in Normandy with the 12th Lancers; Hugh succeeded him as the 7th Baronet and pursued the Germans thereafter with even grimmer determination. We became firm friends.

The first battle that I was remotely involved in was the capture of Arezzo on about 15 July. It was not a particularly drawn-out affair as the Germans were continuing their steady retreat to the Gothic Line, farther north in the mountains. For the next few weeks 1st Guards Brigade acted as the right flank of 6th Armoured Division, part of 13th Corps, pushing up the Arno valley in a series of small skirmishes, while the New Zealanders and others pressed on to Florence, which was finally captured on or about 5 August.

While we were at a place called Quarata the King visited the front line and about half the battalion were lined up for his inspection. It was very hot and he drove slowly past standing up in a jeep, looking very pale; I learnt later that he had been suffering acute diarrhoea during the whole of his visit, poor man.

At this same place Sam Hall was killed. He had taken a patrol out to see if a particular farmhouse was occupied by Germans; one of his men was wounded and it was while bandaging him up that a sniper got Sam in the head.

We usually managed to get hold of fairly undamaged farmhouses during this time and I recall one particularly large and comfortable one at a place called Montevarchi, on the banks of the Arno. It was here that I devised a crude but very effective method of catching fish on a fairly large scale. I got six or eight camouflage nets off the trucks, tied them together and strung the resulting trawl across the river before walking a hundred yards or so upstream where I chucked in a couple of slabs of gun-cotton on a short fuse. We usually gathered in enough fish to feed the entire company, a welcome change from 'compo'. Unfortunately, Joceleyn got wind of my activities and delivered a severe rocket, saying it was misuse of army equipment.

The Arno was a pretty unattractive sluggish river at that time of the year, but in the heat the guardsmen bathed whenever duties allowed. One of Hugh's sergeants, Pheysey by name, suddenly became ill and was taken off to the advanced dressing station. He had contracted

Weil's disease, spread by rats' urine in the water, and when we went to see him two days later he had lost an incredible amount of weight, indeed he only just survived. That put a lot of us off swimming.

The battalion was still well below strength, after the losses of Piccolo and later battles, and so we were joined at about that time by a Grenadier company commanded by David Willis. We were well established across the Arno in a huge villa called Torre-a-Monte; one of David's subalterns, Humphrey Leake, took out a patrol and was badly wounded, dying the next day. Robin Compton, was, I think, also in the same company, a tall cheerful figure. One night Hugh asked me to go and visit one of his machine-gun sections about half a mile from the villa and I decided to borrow a motor-bike, filling the two panniers with tomatoes and fruit. I had got to within a hundred yards of this forward position, no lights of course, when I suddenly found myself flat on my back in the track, with the bike on its side making an awful roar. Switching the infernal thing off, and deciding that it was not after all an ambush, I pushed on gingerly to the farmhouse; when I got inside, into the light, Sargeant Tumelty greeted me with, 'Well, sir, looks like you've cut your bloody throat!' I subsequently learnt that our signallers had laid a line that evening and, crossing the track, had conveniently left the cable at a height all but to decapitate me.

Torre-a-Monte was so solidly built that advanced battalion headquarters ('Tac HQ' for short) was little troubled by the sporadic German shelling and we had one of our frequent impromptu concerts, a highlight of which was a duet by Dick Kingzett and Tom Duboisson, 'If you knew Susie like I know Susie'. Another regular feature of these occasions was a turn by Sergeant Shiers, of the carrier platoon, and consisted of a lengthy (and eventually total) striptease, with words something like:

> Now this old coat of mine,
> The inside is quite new,
> But the outside has seen some stormy weather;
> I'll cast this coat aside,
> In case we get some more . . .
>
> *Chorus*: For all the times we've had together.

I leave the succeeding verses to the reader's imagination.

These occasions would be accompanied by an enormous consumption of rough Italian Chianti (we were only a mile or so from the main Ruffino plant at Pontassieve) which the guardsmen drank like beer out of their pint-sized mugs, without apparent ill-effect.

At this stage of the war in Italy both sides seemed to suffer a depletion of their forces, the Germans more so. Several American divisions had been diverted to bolster the 'Anvil' landings in the South of France, while the Germans were under intense pressure on two fronts. At the end of July the crack Herman Goering Division had been withdrawn from 10 Corps front and was rumoured to be on the way to the Russian theatre of war. We were very well served by various Italian partisans, who managed to slip across into German-held villages and come back with valuable information on troop movements; deserters from the enemy were also a good source of identifying which units we were facing. One of the partisans, Monte Maio, I recall, became more or less permanently attached to No. 3 Company commanded by Bruce Goff, who had occasionally to curb his enthusiasm for letting off a few rounds at the enemy without being asked.

By early September we had worked our way farther forward and started up the valley of the River Sieve, to Dicomano. We now encountered the beginnings of the much vaunted Gothic Line, which Kesselring had been determined to hold at all costs. My platoon had a busy few days lifting mines – we cleared over a hundred and twenty in one morning, I remember – but a lot of the elaborate defences had already been abandoned. Keith Jones took a patrol to the top of Monte Peschiena (four thousand feet) expecting to find the Germans gone but was hit by a Mauser bullet and taken prisoner. (Two of our little airborne party gone . . .)

A day or two later Philip Brutton and I had a lucky escape when we were doing a little 'swanning' on our own and suddenly found ourselves in a small minefield of 's' mines. These charming devices were the size of a large tin of baked beans and contained some three hundred pieces of shrapnel. When they were buried there was little to see of them other than three small prongs; once one was trodden on, there would be a two-second delay before the thing jumped like a jack-in-the-box five feet in the air and exploded. The Germans frequently sowed them on a roadside in combination with a Tellermine (anti-tank weapon). The latter would explode under the weight of a tank, blowing off the tracks; the crew (or survivors thereof) would jump out on to the verge and tread on an 's' mine. I had seen the result of this only a week or so before. Anyway Philip and I tiptoed out somehow in one piece. Not very many days later I was with David Gibson-Watt when we found ourselves in the same situation, but again spotted the wretched things in time.

It must have been at about this stage of the war that the Germans introduced the Schue mine. This was made entirely of wood, except for the detonator, and therefore very difficult to pick up with a mine detector. It was very simply activated by pressure and, although containing only a small amount of explosive, quite sufficient to blow your leg off.

The Germans were quite ruthless in setting booby traps. A few weeks after the events described above I was on Monte Battaglia with Sergeant Williams looking at a dead German face down on the path. Williams was just about to turn him over, to check what unit he was from, when I stopped him. There was something about him that looked wrong; I poked about in the soil underneath his body with a bayonet; sure enough there was a Tellermine, upside down, and with a trip-wire from the subsidiary fuse to the middle button of his tunic.

At the end of September the whole of 1st Guards Brigade was withdrawn from the Pratomagno area and had a brief respite before moving up into the mountains north of Florence. I cannot do better than quote 'Squiff' Ellis's description in *Welsh Guards at War* of what lay ahead of us:

The Welsh Guards went on to Battaglia on 2 October . . . They remained in this sector till the middle of the following February . . . Unlike the armies of bygone days, which at this time of year would have retired sensibly to winter quarters, they continued to man what must surely be one of the most fantastic winter lines ever devised for the discomfort of the troops.*

* L. F. Ellis, *Welsh Guards at War*, Gale and Polden, 1946

94

Monte Battaglia was at the end of a narrow ridge running north-east, and the castle, or what was left of it, stood at over two thousand five hundred feet. The 88th US Division had captured it a week before and had driven off seven counter-attacks with very heavy casualties to both the Germans and themselves. Bodies littered the mountainside, mingled with abandoned weapons and food supplies. To make matters worse the weather broke just as we relieved the Americans and it poured incessantly. Such tracks as there were soon became watercourses and not even the versatile jeep could get very far. We soon became totally dependent on mules for food, ammunition and water.

I took my platoon up the hill soon after we arrived to try and improve some of the tracks, and apart from getting mortared, achieved very little. Thereafter I found myself attached to battalion headquarters helping out where I could. Teal Ashton arrived to take over as second-in-command from Robin Rose-Price, who went to a staff job, and was clearly a weapons fanatic. He would scour the mountainside for German or American weapons and spend happy hours taking them to pieces and cleaning them. The K-rations issued to American troops were scattered everywhere and when we could we organised fatigue parties to pick them up and distribute them among the guardsmen, who were quite delighted with the lavish variety of rations our allies enjoyed. We must have fed on K-rations for several days. I was given two days' leave in Florence after we had been on Battaglia for a week and therefore just missed the only German counter-attack that was made on 1st Guards Brigade, on the night of 10–11 October.

The Grenadiers were at the time holding the castle and heard the Germans approaching in some force; they alerted our No. 3 Company who gave them a very warm reception when they came near enough. They then tried to approach the ridge behind the castle and were severely dealt with by No. 1 Company, retiring to a farmhouse further down. After half an hour nearly a hundred appeared with a white flag and surrendered.

This considerable success was marred for us all an hour or so later when John de Rutzen was killed. Jocelyn had told John to go and see if all was well with No. 1 Company after the surrender and he and

Kemmis Buckley walked along the ridge. On the way they met this large contingent of prisoners, whom John insisted on calling to attention in his best German and generally haranguing. A few minutes later a shell killed John, but miraculously just stunned Kemmis. The gun responsible was without doubt one we had become accustomed to call 'Bologna Bess'; it was clearly of a very large calibre and had a range of at least fifteen miles – probably a naval type of weapon on a railway track. John's death was a severe blow to the entire battalion, with whom he had been since its formation and who held him in high esteem and great affection.

Many years later, down in Pembrokeshire, I was told a curious story. At a certain date in the nineteenth century the de Rutzen of the day decided to build a new and much larger church and closed the old Church of St John of Jerusalem at Slebech. This was much resented by the parishioners and one old woman, probably of gypsy blood, cursed the family, saying that 'when the gates to Slebech fall, that will be the end of the de Rutzens'.

On a very stormy day in October 1944, the chief constable had some business with Johnny Philipps (John de Rutzen's brother-in-law) and was on his way to Picton Castle, with a superintendent. As they passed the Slebech entrance they were horrified to see one of the gate piers toppling over; two days later Sheila, John's wife, received the telegram announcing his death, which had occurred on the 11th, the same day as this incident. Sheila had an infant daughter, Victoria, but no son and the de Rutzen line was ended.

During all these stirring days in the mountains the battalion had two redoubtable 'camp followers', who cheered us up enormously. Lorna Twining, whose husband Dickie had been killed at Fondouk, and 'Gypsy' Lawrence;* they operated a fifteen-hundredweight truck which was a mobile dispenser of 'tea and wads', and everywhere that 3rd Welsh Guards went, Lorna went too. She and Gypsy were quite intrepid and I recall Andrew Scott ordering them farther back on more than one occasion. Lorna was a most attractive and vivacious woman; at the end

* the late Lady Charles, widow of Sir Noël Charles

of the war she married Desmond Chichester but sadly died giving birth to their son.

It was not surprising that the Germans had made such determined efforts to recapture Battaglia, first from the Americans and then from 1st Guards Brigade; the castle dominated the whole area. After the war was over, I recall going to Bologna for the weekend from Fano and that unmistakable, forbidding finger on the high ridge was clearly visible from there, an easy target for artillery. After the abortive German counter-attack described above, Colonel Jocelyn told me to lay some trip-wires out in front of the castle in case they tried again; it was the only time I went up there and a very messy business it was too. The approach was as steep as a pitched roof, the mud was like molasses and there were numerous unburied Germans to fall over in the dark. Henry Cottam was holding the feature at the time and was totally unperturbed at his responsibility. Henry won a well-deserved Military Cross a few weeks later, on Monte Verro, and after the war returned to his great love, medicine, but was sadly to die in a motor accident.

I suppose we were on Battaglia for about three weeks in all, before being switched to the other side of the Santerno valley. Here 3rd Welsh Guards came briefly under the command of 36 Brigade, part of 78th Division, in a very unpleasant place called Sassaleone, which was burning merrily when we arrived. Colonel Jocelyn was pretty unhappy about our situation there but after he had words with Andrew Scott, commanding 1st Guards Brigade, we were able to rejoin our usual companions.

It was now the end of October and we settled down to a routine that could only be compared to what troops did in the 1914–18 War. We would do five days in the line, then five days in our rest area, alternating with the 2nd Coldstream (the 3rd Grenadiers had gone somewhere else). For three and a half months we held the same bit of mountain, called Monte dell' Aqua Salata, with an adjacent ridge called Verro. To reach these positions involved a six-mile trudge, from Fontanalice, down in the valley, up narrow muddy tracks that became worse every week as the weather deteriorated further and the mule trains churned up the mud. Jo Gurney was in charge of the mules and did a wonderful job. Some of the muleteers, who were of various nationalities, had to be kept at it since it was an unpleasant and hazardous job; apart from constant shelling (and once the line had got bogged down, each side knew pretty accurately where the other's supply lines were), the mules frequently lost their loads or got totally stuck in the mud with their four rather pointed hooves, whereupon they invariably passed out from fright or exhaustion.

I spent most of this time at Tac HQ where, apart from Colonel Jocelyn, with whom Teal Ashton alternated, there were, among others, Elydr Williams, commanding HQ Company, Tom Dubuisson and Dai Morris, our battalion medical officer. Dai was a native of Portmadoc and an imperturbable character who had a very robust attitude towards soldiers' complaints, whether real or imaginary. Unless they were obviously *in extremis* Dai would just prescribe 'medicine and duty', for which he earned the sobriquet 'Dai M & D'. Tac HQ was in a farmhouse called Carre on the reverse slope of Aqua Salata; it was a pretty solid structure and during the whole time we were there never received a direct hit, fortunately.

As the winter came on and snow began to fall and lie on the hills (we were at the two-thousand-feet level) we were issued with extra clothing including white snow-suits which made it more difficult for movement in daylight to be detected. Another innovation, which greatly helped when one battalion was relieving another, was 'artificial moonlight' created by powerful searchlights sited in rear positions which reflected off the clouds.

Nothing could be more of a contrast to all this than our rest area south of Florence, at Greve. Here, in the heart of the Chianti district, we took over a large *castello* and some adjoining houses; after a long and bumpy drive back from the line it was bliss to shed one's filthy battledress and have a good night's sleep. Refreshed, we would then fall on any mail that had come from home, sometimes with a welcome parcel, and then drive into Florence, twelve miles away, for a bit of light entertainment. Apart from the bridges across the Arno, all of which the Germans destroyed except for the Ponte Vecchio, the city was undamaged and most of the hotels and a lot of restaurants and some night clubs were still functioning. Hugh Arbuthnot had an elderly cousin who lived in Florence with her married daughter, a Signora Capponi, and a very beautiful eighteen-year-old grandaughter, with whom half the battalion were immediately in love. Mrs Arbuthnot's house was in one of those streets that runs down to the Arno, the Via Bardia, adjacent to the Ponte Vecchio, and while the Germans still held the city she watched them laying mines from her drawing-room window. When they had gone and the first New Zealanders arrived she went out to greet them and with her parasol indicated exactly where each mine was laid. She was then eighty and lived to be just a hundred. Going to afternoon tea there was like stepping into an English country house.

We made lots of other friends among the Florentines and I have the happiest memories of that beautiful city, which is always a joy to re-visit. In the winter of 1944, however, I fear we pursued little culture; apart from the fact that all the museums were shut and the pictures hidden away in places like the Sitwells' Montegufoni, our short visits were strictly concentrated on wine, women and song. I recall one night when Bob Sale (who had taken over Support Company after John de Rutzen had been killed) was driving a party of us back to Greve, missed a turning, and took us at speed round a bank rather like the 'wall of death' – successfully, because we were about nine strong in the jeep and sheer centrifugal force kept it upright.

Meanwhile, back at home everyone was coping as best they could. Valerie was living at Bickley with a six-month old baby and cheerfully wrote to me about the V2 rockets, 'at least if you hear the bang you know it's landed somewhere else!' My mother was dug in at Owlswood, with Uncle David still conducting courts-martial from an office in Spring Gardens, and my father was in the fifth month of a long fight against tuberculosis in a sanatorium near Denbigh. He was a faithful correspondent and I still have a lot of his letters from this period. They were mostly typed, on airmail forms, as he found he could get more on the page that way.

He had been greatly preoccupied with completing his book on Nain, *Dame Margaret*, which finally appeared the following year; on 23 December he wrote:

I have not heard yet whether my manuscript has arrived in London safely, but I am half expecting Mrs Jenkins [the lady who took it up] to call in today so I may hear. It has been most interesting reading about our old ancestors and it makes you feel proud to think that you and I are descended from such a man as Owen Gwynedd. He undoubtedly was one of the great figures of the twelfth century and he gave Henry II such a smack in the eye in 1165 near Llangollen that the Normans left Wales alone for about a century and a half after that. He must have been a very fine soldier, because the weakness of the Welsh always had been that although they had plenty of guts and dash, they were sadly lacking in steadiness and discipline, and he seems to have moulded them into a very fine fighting force. He was also a great patron of the bards, and some of our finest singers, such as Gwelchmai, flourished at his court. By the way, after his death one of his sons settled down at the place where Valerie was born, Tal-Hen-Bont, three miles from Criccieth. When we were there it was called Plas Hen, but the owners reverted afterwards to the old name.

I found these philosophical disquisitions from my father strangely comforting amid the uncertainty and general discomfort that was our normal lot in Italy.

Taid had left Churt for the last time in September and moved up to Ty Newydd, at Llanystumdwy. He had in fact bought this Jacobean house before the war but had never spent a night there; now it was got ready for his last days, back in the village of his boyhood, with Frances as his devoted companion and nurse. AJ wrote in his diary for 21 September 1944:

In the course of a discussion with Sir Thomas [Carey-Evans] he made a remark to me. He said that he would not be surprised if LG's instinct had not led him to his old home to die, like an old dog returns to his lair.*

---

* A. J. Sylvester, *Life with Lloyd George*, p. 329

Taid with Megan above the Dwyfor, a few yards from his burial place

A week after the letter from my father quoted above he wrote to me again intimating for the first time that Taid had accepted a peerage. Before I received this however I recall Jo Gurney, who had picked up the BBC news on 1 January, jocularly informing me that I was now a future earl!

Very briefly, the sequence of events had been as follows. It was obvious by the autumn that the end of the war was in sight and that therefore an election could not be far away (there had not been a General Election since 1935). It was equally obvious, painfully so to those closest to him, that LG would not be fit enough to fight such a campaign, that the electoral composition of Caernarvon Boroughs had changed materially in the past decade and that after fifty-five years as the member it would be a humiliating blow for him to be defeated.

In the first instance, therefore, AJ was dispatched to London (he had been in attendance at Ty Newydd all autumn) to sound out senior representatives of both Tory and Labour parties with a view to obtaining a 'walk-over' for LG. While sympathetic, neither party could guarantee that their local associations would agree to such a proposal. AJ recorded what happened then:

> My next commission was to make a move in the most diplomatic manner somehow to bring to the attention of the Prime Minister that LG might be even willing to consider an earldom. It had to be a very delicate approach; knowing the close personal relationship between Archie Sinclair and Winston, the Prime Minister, and that Archie was leader of the Liberal Party, I visited his office in Whitehall, where he was Secretary of State for Air. I was met by Mr Maudling, his private secretary, and ushered into the room of the Secretary of State. Archie gave me a very warm and sympathetic hearing when I discussed with him the possibility of an earldom being offered to LG, by the King, for political and health reasons. I explained that although there was no certainty that LG would accept, it would give him immense pleasure. Archie promised to speak to Winston. I reported fully to LG by memorandum and telephone.

There was a good deal of amazement expressed at the time that David Lloyd George, the great commoner and in his prime the most vigorous scourge of the House of Lords, should have accepted a title. Some people, including members of the family, leapt to the conclusion that he had been unduly influenced in his decline by Frances, who was supposed to find the prospect of becoming a countess alluring. But I think myself that, realising his active days as a House of Commons man were numbered, he wished to retain a platform from which to make his views felt and continue to exert some influence. As he left no written memoranda on the subject, any view is purely speculative; the simple fact was that by the time he came to die, he had created a dynasty.

But in January 1945 all this seemed to me a long way off and of little significance when compared with staying in one piece on the snowy wastes of Aqua Salata and Verro, to which we returned with relentless regularity. Corps HQ ordained that there should be a full-scale battalion attack from these positions, but Andrew Scott, commanding 1st Guards Brigade, managed to persuade Corps that it would be totally unproductive and it happily never took place. I did not go 'up the hill' every time; at one stage, I was sent on a course to learn all about flame-throwers, and had to demonstrate what I had learnt to the battalion on my return. The equipment bore a strong resemblance to that which one now uses for spraying weeds. Mounted as a backpack, it comprised a lifebuoy-shaped container which held inflammable gunge; inside this was a small sphere of compressed air from which a tube led to a hand-held gun which ignited the stuff from a torch battery. It was incredibly makeshift and a bullet or piece of shrapnel in the cylinder would make very short work of the aspiring thrower of flames. I only saw them in action once, at a considerable distance, when the Rifle Brigade were attacking a village called Tossignano on our right.

In about mid-February we came off the mountains for the last time and thankfully moved down to Spoleto, where we joined up with 24th Guards Brigade for a general shake-out. My platoon sergeant, 'Wog' Hughes, had the bright idea of making a small museum display of mines and other devices for the edification of the guardsmen. While I supported the idea wholeheartedly, I was not quite prepared for some of his methods. For safety we thought we should remove the explosive from the mines and I found Sergeant Hughes one morning with a Tellermine wedged between his knees, going at it furiously with a steel hammer and cold chisel, sparks flying in all directions. When I remonstrated and pointed out that it seemed a pity to blow ourselves up now, having survived so much, he relented and took to steaming out the explosive. The display proved a great success.

Spoleto, set in the Umbrian hills, was an attractive place to be in, and as February ran its course the sun started to shine. We celebrated St David's Day in fine style, with lots of singing at our morning service and plenty to eat and drink later. I remember Malcolm Richards offering up a prayer for my old grandfather at the service, which embarrassed me somewhat, though it was well meant as he was clearly in his final days.

In mid-March we moved across to the Adriatic to a small fishing town called Porto San Giorgio, where serious training for the final spring breakthrough began. I was on one of these exercises when a dispatch rider told me that the brigadier wished to see me; my heart sank as a few days earlier I had been one of a party who had 'beaten up' a place called Macerata, incurring the wrath of the town major, and I fully expected that this particular chicken had come home to roost.

Not at all. I saluted Brigadier Andrew, who said he was sorry to hear about my grandfather (he had died two days previously) and told me, 'You are to fly home.' I gulped in astonishment and he went on, 'Nothing to do with me. I have here a VIP signal from Caserta [Allied Forces HQ] and you must be off in half an hour.'

Winston Churchill, in the midst of conducting a great war, had been inspired to think that it would be a fine thing for the four grandsons of his old friend and political ally to be at his graveside, and had accordingly issued the necessary instruction. I was the farthest afield; David was firing his 5.5s across the Rhine, Robin was flying a bomber nightly from a home base, and Benjy was in the North Sea in HMS *Enterprise*.

Within half an hour I was flying in a fighter from Senegallia down to Naples, where I stayed the night in Field Marshal Alexander's villa (he was away); the following morning I flew to London in a bomber. Though I did not know it at the time I had heard my last shot fired in anger.

CHAPTER 9

Taid's Funeral and Aftermath

Taid's last weeks had been a period of steady decline; although in no pain, he slept a great deal and his bed had been moved into the library of Ty Newydd, from which he could look at the view over Cardigan Bay. Frances nursed him devotedly. In a letter to Lord Dawson on 26 February, Dr Prytherch, the Criccieth family doctor and a good friend to us all, wrote: 'His wife is doing a grand job of work . . . she is doing it with all the devotion he deserves, and she is doing it unstintingly and extremely well, and he calls for her constant presence; one cannot say more than that he is one of the best-cared-for patients I have ever had.'

He could still surprise everyone. One day when Robert Prytherch was with him he asked what he had been doing that morning; Robert said he had been to see a patient near Chwilog and mentioned the name of the farm. 'Oh yes,' the old man said with a twinkle, 'I used to know a girl up there'. On another occasion he opened one eye and said to Frances, quoting one of his favourite poets, Robert Burns, 'Am I no' a bonny fechter?'

Megan and Olwen came over from Brynawelon regularly and there was, for the time being, an uneasy truce between them and Frances. Writing to me on 7 March, from the Lion Hotel, Criccieth, AJ had said: 'You will be interested to know that Megan's attitude to Frances has undergone a radical change and she is now polite!' They were all at his bedside, together with AJ and Jennifer, Frances's daughter, as well as the faithful Lallie, when he drew his last breath on the evening of 26 March.

As recounted in the previous chapter, I was flown back from Naples in a bomber and spent the night in London. Early next morning, Good Friday, I was out at Northolt and climbed into a Hurricane for the final leg to North Wales. The pilot was a Pole, and more accustomed to low flying sorties over France than trips to North Wales; I was a little worried to see that his only navigational aid appeared to be a small Phillips' school atlas. Somewhere over Cheshire he decided we would not have enough fuel to do the easy route over Liverpool Bay and thus to Anglesey and so made a sharp left turn towards the mountains. Visibility was poor and the next twenty minutes were hair-raising as we threaded our way through the Berwyns and peaks of Snowdonia before we finally touched down at Valley airfield.

I arrived at Ty Newydd only an hour before the funeral. The little lane up from the bridge at Llanystumdwy was already full of people, with many more converging on the village from all directions.

There was a short service in the library, just the family standing around the coffin, and then, when it had been taken down and placed on a farm wagon drawn by a single shire horse, we went slowly down the drive and to the spinney above the river. He had chosen the place with great care; it was directly above the River Dwyfor, tumbling urgently below, with wonderful views to Snowdon beyond. A last-minute hitch had nearly wrecked the arrangements as no one had thought of consecrating the site, but this had been done early that morning by one of the clergy.

As David, Robin, Benjy and I walked beside the coffin to the graveside we were met by an amazing and very moving spectacle. There were literally thousands of men, women and children thronging the lane and on the steep hillside around the grave, with thousands more in the meadows just across the river. The singing started as the cortège approached; many of Taid's favourite Welsh hymns – 'Llef', 'Tyddyn Llwyn' (Cottage in the Spinney) and of course 'Cwm Rhondda' – all sung with immense fervour under the leadership of Mr Matthew Williams, from Anglesey. No true Welshman could have remained unmoved and it was just the right send-off for one who had done so much for his own people and who had chosen to be buried among them, amid the scenes of his boyhood, rather than in the pomp of the Abbey – 'parmi ce peuple que j'ai si bien aime' (among this people I have loved so well), in common with Napoleon.

I have little recollection of what happened immediately after the funeral – we were all emotionally drained, I suspect. I know that although I stayed the night at Ty Newydd I had supper at Brynawelon, and someone must have given me a lift to London. It was Easter and I had a relaxed weekend with my mother and Uncle David at Owlswood before reporting to regimental headquarters. Brigadier Sir Alexander Stanier DSO, MC had succeeded Bertie Bankier as our lieutenant-colonel; I had already met him once when he visited the battalion in Italy; Sammy Stanier, as he has always been known, was the first Welsh Guards officer to join the regiment directly from Sandhurst in 1917. (Until then we had been formed almost entirely out of Grenadiers.) He gave me two weeks' leave, then I had to report to Sandown Park preparatory to getting back to Italy, hopefully before the war was over.

The following week there was a packed memorial service in Westminster Abbey and a smaller one in the Welsh Church in Castle Street which Taid had always attended when he was in London. After these formalities were over, I headed back to North Wales to see my father who was still in the sanatorium near Denbigh. I found him physically much better and mentally very alert but in a state of impotent rage over Taid's will, from which he had been totally excluded.

In a will of 1935 my father was left five thousand pounds, but this was removed by a later codicil, which stated that 'he had made ample pecuniary benefit for his eldest son during his lifetime', or words to that effect. This could not be denied, since my father had had his debts met on more than one occasion; as I have described in an earlier chapter he had a marked capacity for getting through money and one of his favourite expressions was an adaptation of Mr Micawber – 'Something may turn up.'

But my father's anger now was based on the fact that an entirely new set of circumstances had arisen, namely the creation of an earldom, which was now his, but without a penny to support it. Moreover, he felt that, even if he should receive nothing, it was unfair that no provision whatsoever should be made for the future holders of the title. A year or two previously, when he was still at the War Office, he was in a pub in Baker Street when he came face to face with a man who appeared to be his double. They got into conversation and it transpired that the stranger was indeed an illegitimate son of Taid, and was in receipt of a pension of four hundred pounds per annum for life. Recollecting this did not improve my father's feelings on the matter.

Wills are of course notorious for causing bitter family disputes and this one was a classic example. There was the second wife, who had been his mistress for thirty years; the daughters, who disliked her heartily, one of whom (Olwen) was also excluded; and the eldest son, who was disinherited. The only one of us eight grandchildren mentioned was the youngest, William, who received the farm at Churt, though it was to be held in trust by Megan during her lifetime. The house there and adjoining policies were left to Gwilym, with the contents, though it turned out that Frances had virtually removed all the latter to Ty Newydd. Although she and Megan shared his residuary estate it was Frances who took the major share, as she was bequeathed all the 'chattels', which included an extensive range of freedoms from many quarters of the globe and also his immensely valuable collection of state papers. These covered his entire period in office, from the Board of Trade in 1906 to 1922, and included notes of cabinet meetings, highly confidential letters and memoranda of every sort. Today, no prime minister would be permitted to accumulate such material, it would be firmly retained by the state. Frances sold these papers to Lord Beaverbrook within two years for twenty thousand pounds; they had a somewhat erratic history thereafter. The 'Beaver' first presented them to the University of New Brunswick, his home town; then, having been inspired to create the 'Beaverbrook Library', he brought them back to England, leaving the said university with photostat copies, and the originals remained in Fleet Street until after his death. Max Aitken, his son, finding the running of the library an insupportable burden financially, presented them to the library of the House of Lords. Their final resting place has a certain irony but they are looked after immaculately and of course are readily available to historians and students.

Although Frances tried for a short period after Taid's death to establish herself as the dowager countess at Ty Newydd, it was not a role suited to her. For a while she nurtured a grandiose scheme for a foundation or college in Llanystumdwy, and an appeal was launched. All that remains is a rather ostentatious pair of gates, put up in 1947 and destined to lead nowhere. She sold Ty Newydd and retired to the house at Churt which Taid had built for her several years earlier.

But she continued to sell things, right and left. About ten years later I was dining with David Rockefeller in his New York house and admired a Queen Anne writing desk that was vaguely familiar. 'That belonged to your grandfather,' David said quietly.

AJ told me once of an amazing letter he had from a man called, I think, Vines, who was working for Beaverbrook towards the close of his life. He described how Frances called at Cherkley and after lunch produced various pieces of paraphernalia of LG's which she wished to sell. His pocket-book was produced.

A good description of the 'Beaver' followed: 'His pocket-book!' and he roared with laughter and threw it on the floor. She would sell anything; and yet had no idea of money and was quite at sea after LG's death. When she died in 1972 her will was proved at less than ten thousand pounds, which included the value of her house.

My father was determined to fight the will and over the ensuing year or so employed learned counsel in an attempt to establish that 'undue influence' had been exercised over the old man when he made his final dispositions. But it was a hopeless case from the start; there was little or nothing to go on and he received no encouragement from the rest of the family, who were naturally appalled at the prospect of a lot of public washing of dirty linen. I sat in on several of the conferences which my father had with counsel and after one lengthy session we were descending in the lift when he started sneezing, a habit he had shared with Taid. After some seventeen of these explosions he stood breathless on the pavement and remarked, 'Well, that at least is something I have inherited.'

One very good thing that came about from all this was that my father had been allowed to choose the second title, which, as is customary, by courtesy of the King, he bore until he succeeded. Back in January, AJ had come to see him in hospital as an emissary from Taid, who had suggested Viscount Eifion. My father pointed out that Eifion was only one of the boroughs in Caernarvonshire which LG had represented in Parliament for so long and that the other faithful old boroughs, of Nevin, Caernarvon, Bangor, Conway and Deganwy, would feel rather left out. He therefore proposed Gwynedd, which was the old name for North Wales; in addition Taid's bardic name was Llwyd o' Wynedd, and this would give great pleasure in Eisteddfod circles. Finally, and fortuitously, it would mean that in the fullness of time I should become Owen Gwynedd, thus reviving the name of our great forefather and prince who reigned eight hundred years before.

Taid of course never lived to take his seat in the House of Lords. The peerage was gazetted sometime in February, he died on 26 March, so was a peer for little more than six weeks. It therefore fell to my father to be introduced in Parliament which he duly was on 6 June 1945, supported by two fellow earls, Warwick and Birkenhead.

Before leaving this somewhat curious tale of the earldom, the follow-ing is, I think, worth recording. My mother had over the years, maintained a friendly relationship with Frances, who had occasionally brought her daughter Jennifer over to Owlswood. Now that Taid's will had become public knowledge, my mother – direct as ever – telephoned Frances for a chat and expressed her surprise and indeed dismay that no provision had been made for me as the future holder of the title. 'Oh,' Frances said, 'but surely the McAlpine's will look after that!' They never spoke again.

Before my leave was over I had managed another visit to Criccieth and went over to see Clough Williams-Ellis, the architect, at his home at Llanfrothen. Clough, who had served in the Brigade in the First World War, had lost his only son Christopher, killed on Cerasola the previous February. The family had asked him to design Taid's grave and its surround at Llanystumdwy and he wanted me to see his preliminary sketches. It was not an easy task since the site chosen was, as I have already described, at the top of a steep bank; but Clough got it absolutely right first time, as I think everyone agrees who has since been there. It is very simple and absolutely in keeping with the atmosphere of the place, with the large smooth boulder that the old man often liked to sit on, as he watched the river, placed centrally, over his grave.

We celebrated my twenty-first birthday on 28 April with a family dinner party at the Dorchester and two days later I sailed from Liverpool on the *Orontes*, bound for Naples and the battalion. I shared a cabin with Robert Pomeroy and Ralph Anstruther who was in the Coldstream Guards and on his way to a staff job. On our first day at sea I heard on the radio from Germany Admiral Doenitz telling of Hitler's death : 'Die Führer ist gefallen – ' followed by music from *Götterdämmerung*. The following day (2 May) came the news of the unconditional surrender of the German forces in Italy to Field Marshal Alexander. It was obvious that the war was over, and in fact the surrender in Germany came within a week. This did not seem to affect our captain's thinking and we took a huge detour out into the Atlantic before heading for the Mediterranean, reaching Naples on about 10 May.

Stopping at Fano on the Adriatic coast for a week or two, I eventually rejoined the 3rd Battalion in Austria, where they had finally come to rest after a lightning breakout at the Argenta Gap, followed by the crossing of the Po and finally of the Adige, where the Germans had surrendered. Robin Rose-Price was commanding and Christopher Thursby-Pelham was still adjutant; Bob Sale was my company commander and I was reunited with my old platoon.

Life in Austria was very relaxed: apart from the sense of relief that the killing had stopped, the battalion had found idyllic quarters in and around the village of Rosegg, on the shores of the Worthesee, a fifteen-mile-long lake which ended with Klagenfurt at its eastern tip. Battalion headquarters and the officers' mess were in a very elegant *Schloss* that belonged to the local princess, with whom Francis Egerton engaged in diplomatic forays of which he invariably emerged as victor: the only major disaster occurred when the mess sergeant, in a fit of zeal for our well-being, slaughtered the princess's favourite cow. We fed extremely well. The Austrians had not suffered great hardship like the Italians and local supplies were abundant. We had also overrun large German supplies of both food and drink; there was no need to hold back. Nearly every officer in the battalion had managed to lay his hands on a motor-car of some description; Colonel Robin had a super-charged Alfa-Romeo which it was rumoured he had never succeeded in getting into top gear as it did 100 mph in third. I acquired an open German touring car, called, I think, a Stoewer-Ackoner, which one might describe as a poor man's Bentley.

There was also a fine stable of horses, which had belonged to the Cossacks, and Bob Sale soon had us all riding out every morning. These unfortunate Cossacks, who had been taken prisoner *en masse* on the Russian front two years earlier, were duped by the Germans into changing sides with the promise that when they (the Germans) had won the war they (the Cossacks) would be given the Lombardy plain in which to settle. They, and a large number of Yugoslavs of various persuasions, became the subject of a bitter tussle between the hard bargaining of higher command and the consciences of the officers and men who actually had to carry out the distasteful task of returning them to their country of origin, often to certain death, and usually by subterfuge. But as all this had occurred before I rejoined the battalion and as it has been so well documented by those on the spot, I do not propose to discuss it other than to record my belief that it was a shameful act, even allowing for the confusion among displaced peoples that prevailed in 1945. The late Eric Penn, a distinguished Grenadier of the utmost probity, told me that it was the only time in his experience that he had known guardsmen come near to disobeying orders.

Our time in Austria soon came to an end and 1st Guards Brigade began the complicated business of returning home. I say complicated because it was made so by the fact that the liner *Georgic*, which had been earmarked for our return from Naples, was virtually high-jacked by the 6th South African Division, who thought that the war being over they might as well get back to Cape Town as soon as possible. We therefore had to return piecemeal, priority being given to those who had been abroad longest, who were flown home.

Bob Sale and I, and most of Support Company, found ourselves as the rearguard of the battalion, tidying up at Rosegg. This was not very arduous and we managed a trip to Linz I recall, and one or two other Austrian towns. Even more satisfactory, as we were on our way down to the Adriatic, to Fano, we contrived a week in Venice. The city had been completely bypassed by hostilities and gave us that languorous welcome which it has extended to every visitor for centuries. We stayed at the Luna, which had been taken over as the officers' transit hotel, and was extremely convenient for Harry's Bar, where we usually found a few chums. We swam out at the Lido and gambled there in the casino, returning early one morning by gondola which seemed to take about two hours – I hate to think what it would cost today! The town major had put up a large notice halfway up the Grand Canal: 'Motorboats causing excessive wash will be impounded.' Very sensible and a warning that might be repeated with benefit in 1999. I am not quite sure how it arose but Bob had laid his hands on a large roll of carpet before leaving Austria and this was successfully turned into hard cash in Venice, which Bob distributed among every man in the company, with a modest portion to ourselves. This all made for a very happy week and made me a Venice lover for life.

Back in England the inevitable general election had been called and on July 5th the people went to the polls, for the first time in ten years. The outcome was a huge landslide in Labour's favour, which amazed everyone, including Mr Attlee who told Jock Colville that his most optimistic forecast was a modest Conservative majority of forty seats.*
But a new generation had come of voting age during those ten years, a great many of whom were in the forces, and although we had won a long and costly war, the memories of the thirties, when appeasement had helped to make that war a certainty and a national government had dithered and neglected its duties, had left a scar on people's minds which only a total change of leadership could erase. Every officer had to lecture his platoon on the issues at stake and the aims of the three parties; looking back I am amazed that any of us had the presumption to know what we were talking about, but these were orders and we muddled through somehow.

Another recollection of this period is that I obtained, just before returning from the UK, an early copy of *Brideshead Revisited*, which was read avidly by so many of my companions while we were in Fano that it

---

* John Colville, *The Fringes of Power*, Hodder & Stoughton, 1985, p. 611

became very tattered and drink-stained. One of Evelyn Waugh's earlier novels, *Put Out More Flags*, had become almost required reading by young officers in the brigade, so very funny and apt were some of its passages, and certain phrases, such as, 'Now he's getting a rocket', were often repeated with glee at appropriate moments. I had met the author in a night-club in Rome the previous summer, and on learning my name he had been, I thought, unnecessarily offensive about my grandfather; but he was very drunk and, in all probability, so was I.

At the end of July a fairly small party of us, the remnants of 1st Guards Brigade, embarked at Naples on a very dirty little Italian steamer which was to take us to Marseilles on the first leg of our journey home. As well as Elydr Williams, David Wroth and Jim Jerman from the battalion, I remember Bob Southey, a Coldstreamer, Bill Birkbeck and Nigel Nicolson who was brigade intelligence officer.

The current, rather weak, joke was that BLA (British Liberation Army) actually stood for Burma Looms Ahead; this was far from being funny as it was indeed planned that we should have six weeks' leave, get kitted out in tropical gear and sail for the Far East to engage the Japanese. So when on 6 August we learnt that the first atomic bomb had been dropped on Hiroshima, in spite of being in a fierce squall in the Bay of Genoa, we all celebrated immoderately. After being held up for a week in Marseilles, we then took three days by train to reach Dieppe, the only time I have slept in a luggage rack.

Although it was good to be home again – and for many it had been two and a half years – Britain post-war was a dreary place, with severe rationing still in operation and an ominous programme of socialist legislation in the pipeline. The days of the 3rd Battalion were running out, which was inevitably a sadness, for such a unit becomes very much a family and this one in particular had achieved so much in its short life, had lost many good people and was a very proud battalion.

After leave we were sent up to Selkirk in September, where the colonel of the regiment, Lord Gowrie, came to inspect and said nice things about us. Very shortly after this, Colonel Robin left us to go to a staff job and was succeeded by Billy Malcolm. The latter had been taken prisoner in 1940 and, I think, found the rather relaxed attitude of the younger officers in marked contrast to what he remembered from pre-war days. But we all settled down happily and an early bonus materialised one evening when the Duke of Roxburgh came to dinner (he and Colonel Billy had been at school together) and asked some of us to shoot his grouse. A week or so later, Lady Minto gave a party at Minto House, to which half a dozen of us younger officers were invited and had the honour of meeting the two royal princesses.

From the Borders we were soon moved down to some rather dreary barracks at Great Missenden and those of us who still had a year or more ahead before demobilisation began to get postings to either the 1st or 2nd Battalions. In early December I joined the latter at Bensberg, not far from Dusseldorf.

This battalion had been raised just at the outbreak of war, receiving their colours from King George VI in 1940. In May of that year, they were in action for the first time at Boulogne, fighting a rearguard action against an encircling German force which resulted in a large number of the battalion being taken prisoner. One of these was Jim Windsor-Lewis, who subsequently escaped and four years later was in command when the battalion, by then equipped with Cromwell tanks, fought all the way from Caen in Normandy to the heart of Germany, as part of the Guards Armoured Division under General Sir Allan Adair. At a very impressive parade in June 1945 the division had said farewell to their tanks and reverted to their traditional role as infantry.

Jim Windsor-Lewis was still commanding when I joined that December. Much decorated – as well as a DSO and Bar and an MC he was awarded two Belgian and one Dutch decoration – he was beyond doubt one of the most dashing and colourful officers the Welsh Guards ever had, and was a born leader. I was much in awe of him when I arrived but soon found that provided one never let him down he was utterly fair and had a robust, indeed earthy, sense of humour.

My company commander on arrival was Julian Faber, son-in-law of Harold MacMillan; we became great friends in later years when I had gone to Lloyd's, where he became a distinguished chairman of his family firm. I then moved to Michael Leatham's company, which was great fun as Michael had a strongly developed sense of humour combined with some of the quirkiness of his very alarming father, the redoubtable 'Chicot' Leatham, who had been regimental lieutenant-colonel at the outbreak of war.

Tim Consett was second-in-command, and other company commanders included Rhydian Llewellyn, who had been in Tunisia with the 3rd Battalion, and Stephen Holland, purple in the face and always with his hat on at breakfast; David Gibbs was a very efficient adjutant.

At Christmas I was suddenly told that Ralph Farrer and I were to take a platoon of guardsmen to Nuremberg and carry out guard duties at the war crimes trial; we left Bensberg on the 28 December.

CHAPTER 10

The Nuremberg Trials

Ralph Farrer was a very agreeable companion; he had been a troop commander throughout the 2nd Battalion's campaign through France and Germany, had an MC as a result, and was also an enthusiastic shot – fortunately, as we had ample time during our Nuremberg stay to shoot a good deal.

Our duties were far from onerous, since they involved the provision of the ceremonial guard outside the Palace of Justice on every fourth day, taking turns with American, French and Russian detachments, with whom, I am happy to say, our smart Welsh Guardsmen were invariably compared very favourably.

The Palace of Justice had been chosen for the trials because it was one of the few buildings which was still more or less intact in the old city of Nuremberg and had an adjoining very substantial prison. The rest of the old medieval city was, quite literally, devastated; the US Airforce had rained bombs on its buildings, missing the factories which were mostly out in the suburbs. The stench of death and decay hung over the ruins, the survivors gazed malevolently at us, their conquerors.

Nevertheless, it was entirely fitting that Nuremberg should have been chosen as the place for the leading Nazis to stand trial, for it was here that Hitler held his enormous rallies, in the vast stadium to the south of the city, during the 1930s, and where he spelt out unequivocally his 'final solution' to the Jewish question.

The Charter of the International Military Tribunal had been signed by the four great powers, Britain, USA, Russia and France, on 8 August 1945, with the full backing of the newly fledged United Nations. This charter divided the crimes into (a) crimes against peace (b) war crimes and (c) crimes against humanity. There was a fourth indictment, namely 'the common conspiracy', which covered the insidious growth of the Nazi Party during the 1920s and 1930s towards its subjugation of neighbouring states and ultimate goal of world domination, so clearly spelt out in Hitler's *Mein Kampf.*

The trials had started on 20 November 1945, breaking off for the Christmas-holiday period on 20 December, so that when we arrived on 30 November, the proceedings were still at a relatively early stage. There were twenty-two defendants, but this total included Bormann, whose whereabouts since the final days in Berlin the previous April were unknown and who was presumed dead, Ley, who had committed suicide in October, and Kaltenbrunner, who was in hospital, so only nineteen were actually in the dock.

From the visitors' gallery, to which Ralph and I had access virtually every day, we had a dramatic view of the proceedings. We faced the judges' bench, presided over by Sir Geoffrey Lawrence; to the right were prosecuting counsel, of whom Hartley Shawcross and David Maxwell-Fyfe were our two star performers. In the well of the court was a phalanx of defending counsel, and on the left sat the accused, in a dock two rows deep.

Hermann Goering was at the end of the front row, twenty feet or so from where I frequently sat, and I was able to observe him closely. When captured he had been quite obese and heavily dependent on drugs; weaned off these and on a simple prison diet, he was remarkably fit looking. Dressed in an immaculate grey tunic, always well groomed with his dark hair swept back, he radiated confidence and energy even in his present precarious situation. There was no question as to who was the leading personality there; during a break in the proceedings the others would crowd towards him, asking his views on the point being discussed, deferring to his judgement.

His next-door neighbour in the dock, Rudolph Hess, was, by contrast, very apathetic. He appeared to take little interest in the trial and I frequently saw him reading a book for quite long periods. I formed the opinion then that his mind had become unhinged, and nothing later made me alter that view.

Guard mounting at Nuremberg, January 1946

Ribbentrop sat on his left, a frightened rabbit of a man who from being a champagne salesman had become Hilter's ambassador to Britain, and was then so full of arrogance that, when presenting his credentials to King George VI in February 1937, he had given the Nazi salute. He irritated those concerned during the trial by applying for all sorts of improbable people to come and give evidence on his behalf, such as Lords Beaverbrook and Vansittart, and even Lady Astor.

Then came Keitel, chief of staff of Hitler's High Command, the man who ordered not only the shooting of fifty RAF officers who had escaped from a prisoner-of-war camp, but also of those commandos who had paddled their canoes up the Gironde, the 'cockleshell heroes'. He was a nasty piece of work.

But the real horrors to my mind were Streicher, Gauleiter of Franconia and a man of the utmost bestiality, Frank, the 'Butcher of Poland', and Kaltenbrunner, who master-minded Hitler's extermination programme. It is no exaggeration to say that a general miasma of evil seemed to envelop the motley crew sitting impassively in the dock.

Nevertheless, there can be no doubt that they were given a fair trial: they were able to engage the leading counsel from all over Germany, and in some cases, from Switzerland, in their defence. They could call anyone they wished to testify on their behalf, and did so with great thoroughness. Throughout they were treated with the utmost fairness by the presiding judge. Airey Neave wrote some years later:

> The central figure at the Nuremberg Trial, from beginning to end, was not Goering. It was not Hess or Keitel, nor any of the defendants. It was Lord Justice Lawrence. This benign balding figure dominated the proceedings for nearly twelve months. He was a staunch, enduring man, who upheld the traditions – respected by the world, in those far off days – of British Justice. This article of faith may be questioned and derided by latter-day radicals but it deeply impressed the nations assembled at Nuremberg.*

Off-duty, Sir Geoffrey Lawrence liked nothing better than to relax with his wife and family for dinner and dancing at the Grand Hotel; the two youngest daughters, Robby and Jenny, were great fun and we all had some very jolly evenings while they were there.

We shared a billet with several of the interpreters engaged on the trial in a house at Zirndorf, south-west of the city. These interpreters, the best available in Europe, had the exacting task of sitting for half-hour stretches in sound-proofed boxes and rendering the proceedings into the various languages required on the instant; it was an exhausting job but on the whole the system worked well and only broke down on rare occasions. (One of these was many months later, at the moment that Goering was being sentenced.)

One of our companions in the billet was a lively little Pole called Harry Trombala, who had an enormous capacity for alcohol and who formed an unpredictable member of our nightly poker school.

It was from Zirndorf that we set out on our regular forays to shoot duck on the various tributaries of the River Pegnitz and farther afield. We

---

* Airey Neave, *Nuremberg*, Hodder & Stoughton, 1978

enlisted a local *Förster* to organise boar and deer shoots, sometimes successful but usually blank, as the war had disrupted game preservation here, as everywhere else. The Bavarian countryside was delightful, even in midwinter; I especially recall discovering one snowy afternoon the little walled town of Rothenberg, mercifully by-passed by the battles and retaining its medieval appearance.

Even after our tour of duty at Nuremberg was over and we had re-joined the battalion, I followed the trials daily in the press, up to their dramatic conclusion. In August the defendants made their final speeches from the dock and on 1 October, after lengthy deliberation, the judges announced their verdicts and passed sentence. Twelve were to hang, with life sentences for Hess, Funk and Raeder. Speer, in my view leniently treated, got twenty years, and Schacht, the banker, Von Papen and Fritzsche were found not guilty.

Since the US army had been responsible for guarding the prisoners throughout the trials, it was only natural that they should supply the executioner, in the person of Master-Sergeant Woods from Texas. From all accounts he bungled the job and it would have been a more humane affair had our own Albert Pierrepoint been allotted the task. But the most important criminal of the lot managed to avoid his walk to the gallows set up in the gymnasium: an hour before his execution was to take place, Hermann Goering was found dead in his cell; he had taken potassium cyanide.

I heard three theories as to how he had obtained the poison. The first was that he had swallowed it before his arrest in a phial so shaped that it was lodged in a part of his stomach; he had only to give himself a sharp blow and it would break. The second theory revolved around the fact that he always wore on his left hand a fine ruby ring (I saw it myself) which was missing when his body was found; he had perhaps bribed one of the guards to get him the poison in return for the ring. The last theory was that when Emma, his wife, had been allowed to see him on the last day, the phial of poison had passed between them during their final long embrace. Whatever the truth, after his request to be shot had been refused, Goering went in his own way.

In the years that have passed since the Nuremberg Trials, which made a profound impression on me, I have often asked myself if it was right to have held them and what did they achieve. My firm belief is that it was absolutely right for the leading Nazis, at any rate those that were still alive, to be put on trial and not shot out of hand – as was Churchill's wish – and the crucial achievement of the International Military Tribunal was to demonstrate unequivocally the wickedness of the Nazi Party. Step by step, from the overthrow of the Weimar government, the evil growth of Hitler's regime was painstakingly traced. The cold-blooded deliberation that lay behind the methodical and chillingly efficient programme of Jewish extermination was fully documented, testified to by countless surviving witnesses, and shown to the court on film and by way of other horrific exhibits. No revisionist work of the late twentieth century can ever alter the court record of Nuremberg.

Forty-five years later, during the War Crimes Debate in the House of Lords, I said:

> It was the tradition of the Temple which ruled at Nuremberg. There could be no question of mistaken identity. These men were who they were said to be. They sat there in flesh and blood. They were on trial in their own country.

Soon after I had rejoined the battalion we were moved from Bensburg to Lübeck, once the chief city of the Hanseatic League and a flourishing port with trade both from the Baltic and via the Elbe canal. Most of the old buildings had been destroyed by bombing, but we took over a very fine undamaged barracks just outside the town.

Every place of any size in those post-war days had an officers' transit hotel, where itinerant officers doing courses, attending courts martial or performing any other duties that separated them from their own units could be put up. I cannot now remember the name of the hostelry in Lübeck which served this purpose but I am unlikely to forget the month during which I now found myself officer-in-charge there. There was a weasel-faced German manager called Hans, who was supposed to run the establishment, but it was a petite blonde called Heike who provided the fun. Heike was twenty-seven and her full name was the

Countess von Reventlow, since she had married a member of that distinguished Danish family at the outbreak of war, though she was delightfully vague about her husband's whereabouts.

To say we got on well would be a wild understatement. Though not, at twenty-one, a sexual innocent, my experience had been mainly limited to the charms of the Bag o' Nails, plus a very short-lived encounter with an Italian girl in Naples; Heike undertook my further education with great ardour and enthusiasm, though how I coped at the same time with running a hotel I cannot imagine. My faithful soldier-servant, Guardsman Bryn Thomas (2738472), had come with me from the 3rd Battalion, and faced the goings-on with imperturbable composure. His attitude often reminded me of the story of the colonel (Welsh Guards, of course) who, after many years' service abroad, finally retired, having persuaded Jones, his servant, to follow him into retirement, explaining that 'things would be just as they always have been'. They arrived very late at his home in Herefordshire and the colonel, having omitted to introduce Jones to his wife – indeed possibily having forgotten to mention that he had a wife at all – went straight to bed. Dawn came and Jones, as usual, appeared with morning tea. Drawing back the curtains he remarked that it was going to be a fine day, then, swiftly moving round the bed, smacked the colonel's lady smartly on the backside with the words, 'Right, you – back to the village!'

I became very fond of Heike but realised that all good things have to come to an end, and I returned to battalion duties. She unfortunately saw no reason why we should end our romance and kept ringing me in the mess; luckily my successor at the hotel, a Grenadier officer who shall be nameless, managed to console her. But I do recall that when I reported to the adjutant, David Gibbs, after my month's absence, he commented, 'You look different.' He was right, I was.

An assignment of a more serious nature came along a few weeks later when Philip Ward and I were detailed to carry the Regimental and King's Colours in the Victory Parade in London in May 1946. After some frantic training sessions in the square we were considered competent enough to be a credit to the battalion and came over with a contingent of NCOs and guardsmen for this great event. We were under canvas in Hyde Park and made an early start to take up our allotted positions in the parade. I have no idea how many members of all the services, men and women, took part, but it was an immense cavalcade and really very enjoyable. It seemed to take hours before we reached the saluting base, on the St James's Park side of the Mall, where the King, accompanied by the Queen and the two princesses, bowed, and we went on our way; it was very moving.

When we got back to Lübeck Jim Windsor-Lewis saw Philip and me separately and, after complimenting us on our performance in the parade, asked each of us if we would consider making the army a career (we were both 'wartime' subalterns.). I thanked him but said I had a job to return to. Philip, however, said yes, he thought he would like to; he subsequently rose to become the first major-general commanding London District (that is the Household Division) that the Welsh Guards had produced.

Colonel Jim left the battalion soon after this and was succeeded by Billy Malcolm. Jerry Spencer-Smith also arrived to take over No. 3 Company, and, just promoted to captain, I became his second-in-command. Jerry was a very unusual character. Having been a most successful and dashing adjutant to 1st Battalion, where he won an MC, he found himself demobilised at the end of 1945 and was encouraged to join the stockbroking firm of his uncle, Ralph Delmé-Ratcliffe. Although he had a very quick brain and was extremely shrewd (his father had been the youngest ever director of the Bank of England), he absolutely hated the City and after three months begged to be allowed back into the regiment. Sammy Stanier, then lieutenant-colonel, who had a high opinion of Jerry's soldierly qualities, agreed and he rejoined without loss of seniority. We became great friends, and he brought a lot of fun into life at 2nd Battalion Welsh Guards. A keen, and very skilful card-player, Jerry established a nightly poker game which went on into the small hours, generally in the room of Harry Webb the quartermaster, with Peter Black and others.

Life in the battalion that summer was very pleasant. At Travemunde there was an excellent club, with very good facilities for sailing. It was

Jerry Spencer-Smith and the author with members of
No. 3 Company, 2nd Battalion Welsh Guards, Lübeck 1947

also quite easy to cross into Denmark, which seemed to have made a rapid recovery from German occupation, and Copenhagen was bursting with every sort of food that we had been without for so long. The Danish girls also seemed very pleased to see us.

But in spite of all these diversions it was still good to get back to the UK on leave, which came round fairly regularly. My father had been discharged from hospital cured of TB, but with only one lung functioning properly, retired from the army. He had never gone back to June but had taken up with an old girlfriend from thirty years before. His finances were, it goes without saying, in a parlous state and he went bankrupt later that year before setting off on a lecture tour in the USA; instead of coming home from there after six months, as had been intended, he stayed there for the next eleven years.

Uncle David was also out of the army and back at the Bar, trying to rebuild his practice in London. My mother had somehow kept Owlswood going throughout the war, isolated as it was, and with only Kelsey to help; as soon as conditions allowed she took to going abroad for a longish spell each winter, several times to South America.

London had a very run-down appearance, with the scars of the blitz only too evident. It was impossible for anyone to do any rebuilding; wild flowers sprang up in great profusion on every bomb-site, redstarts nested in the City ruins, the park railings had all gone to be turned into tanks, and strict rationing remained, of course, in force. But it was still possible to have fun on leave. Edwin and Molly McAlpine were very kind and often gave me a bed in their flat in Park Street: I was also, at about this time, initiated into the mysteries of the Cavendish Hotel and stayed there frequently. Although Rosa Lewis was getting old and let Edith do most of the actual management (such as it was), she still dominated the establishment and liked to hold court in the centre of the hall downstairs and gossip with everyone until all hours, with plenty of champagne, invariably paid for by a bemused visiting American. Rosa had this happy idea that it was only right that the richest should pay, and that impoverished young officers such as myself should have a good time.

Very late one night I was having a drink with Rosa in the little sitting-room to the right of the hall, her own snuggery whose walls were thickly covered with photographs of her patrons and admirers from the past. 'I've forgotten what your father's name is,' said Rosa (I was of course Gwynedd then). 'Lloyd George,' I replied. 'Ah well,' she came back, patting my arm in a consoling manner, 'it's not your fault, dear.' In actual fact Rosa had a perfectly friendly relationship with LG and used to do dinners for him on a regular basis before World War I.

In Germany, later that summer, I was sent to man a control post at Schlutup, where the Russian zone began, on the estuary of the River Trave which flows into the Baltic. We had responsibility not only for manning the crossing point but also for patrolling some six miles of the demarcation line; a neighbouring cavalry regiment took over from there. It was an interesting job; every forty-eight hours a platoon from the battalion arrived to man the position, and I had two interpreters, one of whom, a Pole called Leftcovitch, had fled from blazing Warsaw in 1939, reached England and joined the East Lancs. He was now a sergeant in Intelligence and was invaluable in sifting out the dubious border crossers who came from both East and West. First there were countless Germans who had land in both zones, or had sick and dying relatives on the other side, or who had just found themselves on the wrong side of the fence when the war ended a year before. Then there were the Displaced Persons, Europe's pitiful orphans of the storm, whose wanderings never seemed to cease and rarely brought them home. There were deserters from all armies including our own. And, finally, there were wanted criminals – the black marketeers, large and small, whose nefarious activities took them to and fro, the missing SS men and the professionally violent fugitives from justice who killed and plundered as they went.

I had been there for about a week and was doing a stint in our control post at the barrier, when a German civilian, scruffily dressed, was brought in. His papers seemed in order, but I became aware that Sergeant Leftcovitch was suspicious about the man. He asked my permission to make him strip, and when his shirt was off, told him to raise his left arm. There, in his armpit, was tattooed his blood group, a sure indication that he was SS and on the run. It was typical of German thoroughness that after exhaustive analysis of battle wounds they had settled on this part of the anatomy for recording the blood group of their élite.

It was a strange set-up: two hundred metres down the road was the Russian control post, similarly manned, but we never saw each other or spoke. They had erected watchtowers at regular intervals along the line, permanently manned; within a year the iron curtain had come down with a vengeance and we could feel the suspicion and hostility that emanated from our so recent allies.

The problem of these so-called 'Displaced Persons' was an abiding one and occupied a lot of the battalion's time. In the recent *brouhaha* over the repatriation of Cossacks in Austria in May 1945, I think that people have forgotten, or never knew, the sheer numbers of wretched beings who had either fled from the Germans, or in some cases the Russians, as the war rolled across Europe, and who now wanted to return. Also, as part of the Yalta Agreement, we had undertaken to return Russian nationals when the war ended in return for a guarantee that our own prisoners-of-war in German camps by then in Russian hands would be speedily returned. Many of these nationals had sound reasons for not wanting to return, but they were nevertheless packed off.

I saw numerous boatloads leave Lübeck for Rostock and other Russian ports; the holds had improvised bunks, layer upon layer, and the conditions were appalling. Peter Woods and I had to take a trainload of DPs from Hamburg to Rostock on one occasion. I recall that we lost one passenger before the train left; he gave us the slip by being pushed down the platform in a wheelchair by some friends. After that, whenever the train stopped, and it did frequently, we had guardsmen on the trackside with bren guns until we were moving again. It took two days to reach Rostock and we never slept; coming back in the empty train we stretched out at our leisure, but both got badly attacked by lice as a result.

Towards the end of that summer I was made the battalion welfare officer. I don't know if such an appointment exists in today's army but in Lübeck in 1947 it embraced a fairly wide range of duties, from laying on entertainments for the battalion to trying to sort out guardsmen's personal problems. These not infrequently arose from the activities of an errant wife back at home, and I would be told, 'The wife's done a bunk, sir.' The usual drill in these situations was to contact the local Soldiers', Sailors' and Airmen's Families Association which was invariably helpful.

Equally frequent were cases where a young, unmarried soldier had fallen for a local *Fraülein* and wished to marry her: one had tactfully to point out that we wouldn't be in Germany for ever, that lots of young *Fraüleins* were attracted by uniforms (and the chance of getting some decent food), but it might all look somewhat different back in Swansea, say.

On the entertainment side I remember securing the services of Lale Andersen, the singer who had immortalised the song '*Lili Marleen*' with the Afrika Korps, to perform in the mess. It was not an unqualified success. Miss Andersen was no longer in the first flush of youth and her singing left quite a lot to be desired; matters were not helped by the mess sergeant getting drunk and making a pass at her.

I had more success when I launched an Eisteddfod, with choirs competing from each company, solos both for voice and instrument, and every sort of recitation; this however did not take place until St

David's Day 1947, shortly before the battalion returned to Caterham, as a preliminary to being placed in 'suspended animation'.

That winter, of 1946–7, is one that those of us who lived through it will never forget, whether we were at home or in Europe, for the severity of the weather. In England there was the added misery of an acute fuel shortage. In Schleswig-Holstein the temperature dropped steadily and remained well below freezing for months; the sea was frozen over and it became perfectly feasible to drive across the Baltic to Denmark.

We had some tremendous wild-fowling during those wintry days; the geese were desperate for feeding grounds and duck could be flighted in out-of-the-way streams where there was shelter and some open water. We ate game every night in the mess, including wild boar, which had to be pursued in large tracts of forest, generally driven. The normal weapon for this was a double-barrelled shot-gun, loaded with solid shot (or SG) with a rifled barrel slung beneath, a fairly heavy affair but vital for finishing off a wounded animal. A charging boar, with its hackles raised, is quite an alarming sight, and I have a graphic picture in my mind of Johnny Lloyd-Philipps shinning up a tree with great speed while being pursued by one of these.

Certain officers devised an interesting method of killing boar at night. A bucket of swill was put out, adjacent to a hurricane lamp, and the men climbed into a hide and clamped a rifle so that it was on a fixed sight to the lamp. When the lamp was obscured, the trigger was pulled and one dead boar resulted. Unfortunately, after a few successful evenings, things went wrong when they winged a hungry German who had smelt the swill from afar, and Colonel Billy put a stop to this particular tactic.

I had become very involved with the battalion boxing team and some time in February we got into the BAOR finals which were to be held in Berlin. Jerry Spencer-Smith and I set off in a jeep, with his driver Guardsman Blackman and Guardsman Thomas, through the Russian zone, mile after mile of snowy waste. I recall that we had a puncture, some twenty miles before reaching 'Checkpoint Charlie', in a desolate forest and while Blackman changed wheels we listened to the wolves howling quite near by.

We were in Berlin for nearly a week and although we were unfortunately beaten in the boxing final we had an interesting time and explored what was left of the city. One day we found ourselves in the grounds of the Reich Chancellery, which looked like any other battlefield, pitted with shellholes and littered with burnt-out tanks and other debris, and realised we were very close to Hitler's bunker. At that moment an elderly German appeared, and with the help of Jerry's reasonable knowledge of the language, we got him to offer to take us down. Candles having miraculously appeared (he clearly had done this before), we descended a steep flight of concrete stairs into the bunker itself. It appeared to comprise a lengthy central corridor, off which opened what had been offices, a radio station, mess-rooms, etc. We saw the room in which Hitler and Eva Braun had killed themselves; we also saw Hitler's bathroom, which, like everything else, was stripped bare. I asked our guide where the bath had gone to; he explained that an American major had taken it some weeks before and it was now in his flat in New York! It was an interesting experience, especially as it cannot now be repeated, the Russians having sealed the bunker up and obliterated any trace of the pit near the entrance (which we were also shown) where Hilter's body was allegedly burnt.

Soon after this expedition the wind-down for the battalion's return to the UK began. St David's Day was celebrated with its usual jollities and a visit from the regimental lieutenant-colonel (Sammy Stanier), plus the Eisteddfod, which I have already described. Then the endless checking of equipment and preparations for handing over to another battalion had to be seen to before finally we set out for home, via the singularly charmless ports of Cuxhaven and Hull, and at last arrived at Caterham. On 16 June, the colours were laid up at Windsor and on 1 July the battalion was placed in 'suspended animation', an expression which, nearly fifty years later, has a certain irony. Before this happened I had one more curious experience, which involved taking part in a training film. A Welsh Guards company, commanded by Jerry Spencer-Smith plus myself, John Love and Mark Chinnery, an Irish Guards company, commanded by (I think) Pat Keogh, and a company of Royal Marines were dispatched to the North Devon coast to make a film entitled *Combined Operations*.

We were in Nissen huts overlooking Braunton Sands, near Ilfracombe; the weather had at last improved and the sun occasionally shone and we waited with eager anticipation for our film unit. This proved something of a let-down since it comprised a trio of lugubrious characters with very primitive equipment. The 'director' was an American called Hiram G. Cutts and he proudly announced that he had been making films since the silent days. This was not difficult to believe, but it soon became fairly clear that his experience of military operations was minimal. A lot of DUKW landing craft were assembled and we would fill them up with guardsmen and prepare to let off charges to simulate shellfire; orders would be barked by the company sergeant-major; then Mr Cutts would complain that the sun had just gone in and it would all have to be postponed, by which time half the men were seasick.

After several weeks of this a film of sorts was duly in the can but our hearts sank at the thought that it might ever be used in actually *training* anyone. One possible indirect benefit accrued, though whether this experience was the catalyst I have no idea: Mark Chinnery did in later life become devoted to the film industry.

Sometime in June 1947, I became a civilian again, and collected a motley array of free clothing from a depot near Woking. For the next few weeks I lived a very idle, dissolute life, going to parties, spending too much money and generally regretting the loss of my comrades-in-arms. For this I was chided by my mother, who felt that it was high time I got down to some work.

CHAPTER 11

1947. Back to McAlpine's

I suspect that I was not alone in finding the return to civilian life after four and a half years a traumatic experience, for the army gives one a sense of security akin to that found in a family and the comradeship is constant and comforting whatever the conditions may be. From the privileged position of a captain in the Brigade of Guards, with a soldier servant to look after me, I found myself living on six pounds a week in digs in Wigan. No. 57 Throstlenest Avenue was one of a row of back-to-back houses with a privy in the yard, very limited hot water, but run by a kind bustling little widow called Mrs Thorpe, who fed two young Polish lodgers as well as myself.

Uncle Alfred had died during the war, Jimmie was now chairman of the firm and Alistair Kennedy was managing director. The latter had written to me when I was demobilised inviting me to join the open-cast coal operations in Lancashire. This is how I came to be in Wigan.

Extracting coal by open-cast method became increasingly popular towards the end of the war, and by the late 1940s was contributing nearly ten per cent of total coal production. Many seams of valuable coal lay near the surface and with new and more powerful excavators (especially American ones) it was easy, and of course infinitely safer, to remove the overlying soil and extract the coal. There were inevitably disadvantages to this method, the main ones being that the operation invariably took place over agricultural land, was unsightly and carried mud on to the public roads. Moreover, several years had to elapse before the land could be reinstated and sometimes this was rather poorly done.

Of the larger landowners in the Wigan area, those whose fields we were desecrating were the Bankses of Winstanley. I got to know this delightful elderly couple and had several pleasant days rough shooting as a result. I made other friends in the neighbourhood, but as I couldn't afford a car, life was somewhat circumscribed, especially as the cold weather approached. Wigan in winter has its limitations.

However a number of weekends were made extremely enjoyable, and very amusing, when Jimmie scooped me up at the office on Friday evening and we drove in one of his exotic cars, Lagonda or Bugatti, down to Tickwood in Shropshire.

He had bought this house early in the war, just after marrying his second wife Mary. It was tucked away in a fold of the hills above Buildwas, a few miles from Ironbridge: a brick Georgian house of great distinction with a most seductive atmosphere.

There would usually be shooting on the Saturday, either at Llanarmon or Acton Burnell, a partridge shoot which Jimmie rented. Other guests would regularly include Jack and Daphne Brittain-Jones, John Brocklebank, Pat and Hazel Hall (who lived then at Newport) and Rupert Bibby. The latter was one of Jimmie's oldest friends; they had shared a flat together in Liverpool before the war, after Jimmie had been sent down from Cambridge, and Rupert was considered by Aunt Ethel to be a bad influence. Be that as it may I always found Rupert very entertaining and enjoyed hearing his reminiscences, which concerned, among other things, a spell in Shanghai and wartime smuggling of escapees over the mountains into Switzerland.

The hospitality at Tickwood was on a very liberal scale and Saturday nights were very convivial indeed. I would find my way back to Wigan hungover but happy.

In the spring of 1948 I was moved to North Wales, where McAlpine's were building a number of prefabricated housing estates, mostly in the Chirk area. Our contract was to put in the services, i.e. roads, drains, electricity, etc., plus the foundations for the houses. The latter then arrived by lorry in four sections and were assembled in a matter of hours. They were pretty basic but with the acute shortage of homes at the end of the war they filled a vital need and the sites were generally in attractive locations.

I lived first of all in a pub, the Red Lion (which I saw was shut up just recently) on the A5 near Gobowen, and then got a very comfortable billet with a spinster lady in Chirk who mothered me with tender care, when she was not swooning at the thought of having a real live viscount under her roof. In fact, as far as the job was concerned, I rapidly became known as 'Mr Owen' which suited me very well.

Chirk is a charming town, right on the English border, with the River Ceiriog at the bottom of the hill; this is crossed by two splendid viaducts. One carries the Shropshire Union Canal and the other the main GWR line to Birkenhead. Once, in a first-class compartment, an elderly lady surprised her companion by looking up from her book as the train sped over the great bridge and saying, 'Thank you, Mr Brunel.' She explained that she always said that since the distinguished engineer had built it more than a hundred years before and it couldn't possibly last much longer.

Chirk is of course dominated by its castle, one of Wales's oldest inhabited dwellings and home of the Myddelton family. For many years it was leased by the Howard de Waldens and Uncle Alfred used to shoot there regularly and return hospitality at Llanarmon. The late Lord Howard de Walden once told me of his shock and dismay when, aged about sixteen, he suddenly discovered (on the Myddeltons terminating the lease) that Chirk was no longer his home.

I enjoyed my time in that part of Wales and made a lot of new friends and caught up with others from army days. Cas Jones-Mortimer, who had been taken prisoner in 1940 and spent five years in Germany, was back at his family home, Hartsheath, near Mold, and he and his wife Elizabeth gave me a lot of hospitality. Cas was president of our North Wales Old Comrades' Association and made me chairman. We used to have annual dinners which alternated between Wrexham and Bangor. During his time in prison Cas had applied himself to learning Welsh, mainly from books, and old ones at that. His Welsh was therefore distinctly in the classics mould and it was entertaining to watch the faces of the comrades as he delivered part of his annual speech in Welsh; I doubt if they understood a word but they applauded the effort.

I had acquired a truck of some sort by now so was more mobile and often drove up the Ceiriog valley and explored the Berwyn mountains. Once I got lost near the top of Moel Sych where I knew there was quite a steep drop; fortunately the mist lifted and I found myself within ten feet of the edge.

Shrewsbury was no distance, either by bus or by train, and the Raven (since sadly burnt down) was a good meeting place. I was also frequently over at Tickwood that summer where Jimmie and Mary always made me very welcome. Their daughter Valerie was then about five years old and an enchanting child.

At some point in that year I enrolled as a student in one of those correspondence courses in writing. One had to submit a piece of work weekly and it came back with criticism or occasional praise. Once I had moved on I was too busy to pursue the course, but at the time found it interesting and a challenge, something outside my day-to-day routine.

Early in 1949 I found myself back on open-cast coal, this time as agent for a new site. This meant that I had total responsibility for the contract, which was near Broseley in Shropshire. As it was only a mile or so from Tickwood I cabled Jimmie in South Africa, where he went each winter after shooting finished, to ask if I might be a paying guest there, which he readily permitted. Rupert Bibby was also living there, operating some nefarious timber business from Jimmie's woods, which subsequently ended in recriminations all round. Anyway I was glad of his company and we were thoroughly spoilt by Jimmie's cook/house-keeper Mrs Campbell.

My works manager on the site was a splendid Irishman called Mick Mee who became a firm friend. We had a very good relationship (not always the case between agent and works manager) and we made a substantial profit for the firm.

The area of Shropshire that we were busy despoiling was part of the Willey estate, belonging to Lord Forester. Although the site was to be reinstated in due course the operation was very messy; the laden coal lorries on their way to the weighbridge carrying mud on to the roads, the frequent depredations of neighbouring farms by some of the Irish labourers, and the glare of lights from the nightshift, all made for tricky relations with local landowners. Without however claiming too much credit for my diplomatic skills, I think I managed to establish a good relationship with Lord Forester. At one meeting he indicated that he was quite keen to make a new flighting pond for duck on the estate. In a trice we had a dragline there and a splendid miniature lake was created. I soon found myself asked to shoot, in the formidable company of General Sir Oliver Leese, a redoubtable guardsman and former commander of the Eighth Army in Italy. He was by now retired and had two great interests, his pigs and his cacti.

Even more pleasant was getting to know the Forester family, especially the eldest daughter Christine, who subsequently married Richard Orde-Powlett (now Lord Bolton). Her next sister Juliet was equally attractive and we played tennis at Willey quite a bit. At that time Lord Forester spent part of every year in Rhodesia, where he had a large farm, carried on now I believe by his son.

Looking back now on those post-war days I think that initially I found it much harder to adapt to my job in McAlpine's than I had in 1941, when I left school aged barely seventeen. But adapt I did, and after a couple of years I had found my feet and begun to feel that what I was doing was worthwhile and appreciated. I had very little holiday, a fortnight a year, and spent this either shooting or at Owlswood, with occasional forays to London, where I would meet up with old friends and spend far too much money on late nights.

So I saw very little of my father, whose financial affairs became ever more complicated. He had never gone back to June, who was suing him for various sums, and nothing seemed to go right.

When, in October 1947, he was made bankrupt, it meant among other things that he could no longer attend the House of Lords. As a desperate measure he signed up to do the six-month lecture tour in America already mentioned, and went there before the end of the year. From all accounts the lectures went very well, and he covered enormous distances in between. A number of kind people wrote to me from time to time, prompted, I am sure by my father, to say how well he was doing. The British Consul in Cincinnati wrote: ' . . . your father addressed approximately five hundred people assembled under the auspices of the

University. He received a tremendous ovation at the conclusion of his speech, which was humorous and most interesting.' On St David's Day 1948 he addressed two thousand people in Scranton, Pennsylvania, where, as he put in a letter, 'I heard Welsh spoken as purely as in North Wales.'

Unfortunately, as I learnt much later, my father, with his habitual easy-going attitude to money, received little or nothing out of this tour, an unscrupulous agent creaming off most of the fees. It was a brave effort, but his health was not up to it and by the following year he was up in the Adirondacks, where he took on a variety of jobs – lumberjacking, landscape gardening, etc.

In 1952, he was with an engineering firm when he fell seriously ill with cirrhosis of the liver, the first of renewed setbacks. Finally he got a job with the *Reader's Digest*, where he seemed very happy. During all this time he was living with Anne Andrews, who had followed him out from England, and who devoted the rest of her life to caring for him – not always an easy job.

In March 1958 I had a letter from him, 'I am on my uppers and the balloon has gone up.' He had apparently gone out in 1947 on a diplomatic visa (arranged by Ernest Bevin, then Foreign Secretary) and when this expired after two years had never troubled to do anything about it. He was now told to leave by 10 May, and could I help. The family rallied round, I sent him a ticket on the *Parthia* to Liverpool, met him there two days before my daughter Julia was born and took him to Aunt Olwen at Criccieth.

But I have run on in my narrative and must return to 1949.

CHAPTER 12

Marriage and a Move to Berkshire

Ruth Coit and I first met in March 1945, when I was unexpectedly sent home from Italy to attend my grandfather's funeral. Francis Egerton, then adjutant of the 3rd Battalion, gave me a hurried note to his mother and asked me to deliver it as soon as I could.

After the funeral I was back in London and rang Lady Egerton, who summoned Ruth, her god-daughter, to help entertain a strange young man at her flat in Exhibition Road. Ruth was an only child, born in São Paulo (and still has a Brazilian passport) and had been married in 1940 at the age of twenty-one to an English naval officer in New York. This marriage was annulled within a year. She had then worked in America as part of MI6 (with which her father Dicky Coit was closely involved) and made many American friends, including David Rockefeller. Through the latter she met Walter Rosen, a young US Airforce officer and they became engaged; within a few months he was killed while flying over Germany. Thereafter his parents, Lucy and Walter Rosen senior, treated Ruth as a member of their family.

We did not meet again until three years had gone by, and then in the same flat, where Francis had a small party. Early in 1949 we saw each other a number of times and I took her to North Wales to stay with cousins. In April we became engaged and were married in September, at Holy Trinity, Brompton.

Jerry Spencer-Smith was my best man and helped me through the day with his usual efficiency. Two events stand out in my memory. First, a terrible scene with my mother the night before, when she upbraided me for not telling her that Ruth had been married before, and secondly at our reception at the Dorchester, when Uncle Malcolm, proposing our health and intending to convey to his listeners that he did not know Ruth very well, said, 'Unfortunately I have not had the opportunity to be intimate with the bride.' Rupert Bibby choked on his champagne and had to be helped out.

Thereafter we flew to Paris for the start of our honeymoon. My father-in-law had generously given us a car and arranged for it to be waiting outside the Ritz. As it happened, an old friend from North Wales, Michael Duff, had also been married the day before, to Lady Caroline Paget; the following morning I found him in the car park in the Place Vendôme, no bride in sight and just about to drive off in a jeep with two beautiful young men. Seeing me he said, 'Oh, hello, you're on your honeymoon too – isn't it *marvellous*.'

We went to Zürich and on through the Simplon Pass down to Lake Como and the Villa d'Este, then perhaps the most luxurious of the hotels on those beautiful lakes. I nearly wrecked our new car by driving down from Imola along the Santerno valley, where we had fought four years before and where the roads were still very rough. Then on to Florence and back through France to Paris. Considering the travel allowance was only fifty pounds per annum, it was quite a trip, and largely subsidised by Dicky Coit, who, among other ventures, ran Lunn's the holiday firm.

I had managed to rent a house near Ironbridge, in a pretty village called Leighton, overlooking the Severn valley, and this was our first home. It had been the house in which the author Mary Webb had been born and was the dower house of the surrounding Leighton estate. This had belonged to a family called Kinnersley-Brown but the last member of the clan removed himself to South Africa and, being childless, handed it on to a cousin who was sheep-farming in New Zealand. This cousin, Jemmet Fox by name, and his wife Gwen made quite an impact on the local Shropshire squirarchy, but were extremely kind to us and we enjoyed them hugely. Sadly, they in turn had no children and in due course the estate was sold.

I was making steady progress in the firm and, in addition to being responsible for two open-cast coal sites, I was frequently in the area office at Wolverhampton, presided over by Edmund Jones. Both he and

Jimmie seemed pleased with what I was doing and the latter made it clear more than once that in due course he would like to see me on the board as one of the family.

Unhappily there were influences at work which meant this was never to be. Dicky Coit was determined to persuade me to live nearer to London and exerted himself to this end with great persistence. At the end of December 1949, without my knowledge, he went to see my Uncle Malcolm McAlpine in order to find out if I could be fitted in to the London-based firm. Malcolm very wisely pointed out that whereas Jimmie only had two sons (still both at school) there were already six younger family partners in Sir Robert's and I had a much better chance where I was.

My father-in-law had already made me a non-executive director of Sir Henry Lunn Ltd; late in 1950 he offered me a job with the Miles-Martin Pen Company (which had started manufacturing the Biro pen) at a salary rising from eight hundred to a thousand pounds, more than I was currently earning with McAlpine's. It was a tempting offer but I declined.

The life of a civil-engineering contractor's wife is not a particularly glamorous one; the husband is away during a long day, and though we had a comfortable home and nice neighbours, Ruth undoubtedly found Shropshire life a total contrast to anything she had hitherto experienced. Two things then happened. She became pregnant and her godfather, Alfred Hunter, died and left her a sufficient sum of money for us to buy a house.

My eldest son, David, was born in London on 22 January 1951 and he was christened at Leighton church a few weeks later, receiving the additional names of Richard Owen, so marking the three previous generations of Lloyd Georges.

By midsummer I reluctantly decided to give in to the various pressures that were being exerted and sent in my resignation to Jimmie, who was, quite understandably, extremely disappointed. It was without doubt the silliest decision I have ever made in my life and one that I have bitterly regretted. My mother, needless to say, was incandescent with rage, and wrote to say that I was 'a short-sighted fool' and other stern rebukes, all of which I now accept as well

Brimpton Mill in its timbering days

justified. She disclosed that two years previously, at the time of my wedding, she and David drew up a memorandum under which, if I was still employed by McAlpine's in September 1951, she would buy David a Purdey shotgun; sadly he didn't get it. To conclude this passage on a happier note, twenty years later I was asked to go back to Alfred McAlpine as a non-executive director, which gave me enormous pleasure.

In August 1951 we moved to Brimpton Mill, which Ruth bought for twelve thousand five hundred pounds from Michael and Thalia Gordon-Watson. Michael, who had had a distinguished war with the Irish Guards, was being sent to Washington as Military Attaché and although they had only had the house a short time decided to sell rather than let. The house is delightfully situated on the banks of the River Kennet, which the mill itself, built in 1731, straddles. Originally a corn mill it had been converted to timber cutting early this century, although all the machinery and the huge water wheel had been removed by the time we arrived.

The Mill House, originally Georgian, had been added to extensively in the early 1930s by the previous owners. Sir Thomas Fairbank was an eminent surgeon who specialised in orthopaedics and practised locally in Basingstoke as well as in Harley Street. But it was his wife who saw the possibilities of the mill and who turned its land from a timber yard into an attractive waterside garden, as well as doubling the size of the house. I got to know Kathleen Fairbank quite well as she took to dropping in and she gave us a lot of the local history. Well over six foot, she had an air of great authority, enhanced by the use of a monocle. I subsequently discovered that she was an aunt of Dick Kingzett's; he used to go to Brimpton on days out from Marlborough before the war, and was made to swim in the river.

Her great ally had been Wally Reeves, whom we took on with the property, indeed he was part of it. Born some time towards the end of the last century he had begun work in the timber mill as a boy in 1904, under his father, and knew every nook and cranny of the place. Whether it was the sluice gates or the drains or the water supply or the boilers, Reeves had it all at his fingertips and dealt with every problem in his quiet confident way. For a man who was totally country orientated he had a curious love of crowds and was never happier than when attending some big event. When the Coronation came around in 1953, I arranged for him to go up to London to watch it. A few days later I asked him how he had enjoyed it. 'Nothing like 1911; they fainted like flies then,' was his laconic comment.

One day, in the early 1960s, when Lord Beeching was wielding his axe, there was a commemorative last journey on the Newbury to Lambourn railway line. Wally Reeves went and it turned out that he was the only person aboard who had been on the very first train nearly seventy years before. Apart from his attachment to the mill he was also the local sexton, and occasionally begged to be excused from the garden for an hour or so as there was a grave to be dug or a bell to be rung. He became a staunch friend to us all and continued to bicycle down from the village to the garden until he was well over eighty.

Thalia Gordon-Watson had run a small herd of Jersey cows and I took on her cowman, a Lancastrian called Mitchell, but switched to Guernseys. I bought Wessex Saddleback pigs and crossed them with a

Large White boar, selling the progeny as eight-week-old weaners in Newbury market. In the belief that it would be more profitable to fatten them on until they were ready for the factory, I built a fattening shed (unaided) and housed them on deep litter. This worked well and produced unlimited manure for the kitchen garden, but since I was buying in all their food and straw, there was precious little profit. But I became very fond of my pigs, dear creatures that they are.

I then embarked on chickens and soon had some eight hundred laying their heads off on deep litter in the upper floors of the mill; a light on a time-switch woke them up around two in the morning and in theory encouraged them to lay an egg before going to sleep again before true dawn arrived. I am not sure how ethical this was or indeed whether it really worked – hens are not really as stupid as some would believe.

Finally I bought some three-year-old Welsh mountain ewes from my cousin Benjy and put them to a Suffolk ram. The change from the slopes of Snowdon to the lush pastures of Berkshire had a stimulating effect on their reproductive process and twins were the order of the day. Welsh lamb, as everyone should know, is unbeatable and I could not supply enough to our local butcher.

All this took a fair bit of effort and organisation but I still managed to put in a 'refresher' term of agricultural science and animal husbandry at Reading University, where I had enrolled as a mature student. I learnt a lot from my short time there, especially on the afternoons at the university farm at Sonning.

Fifty years ago that area of Berkshire between Reading and Newbury was still largely rural, with the odd factory at Theale and Reed's paper mill at Thatcham. The Cornish Riviera express still thundered through Midgham station at about 11.20 every morning, headed by a magnificent king-class locomotive, Newbury was still a thriving market town with probably the best one-day agricultural show in England held on a local farmer's field, and the A4, London to Bath, was still a pleasant and easy road to the West.

But there were adverse omens even then. The Atomic Research Establishment had arrived at Aldermaston soon after the war, though to be fair it has never been a problem to the neighbourhood, and Sir

William Penney, later Lord Penney, its first director, firmly declined offers of country houses nearby, opting to live 'on the job' and show people there was nothing to fear. The arrival of the US Airforce at Greenham Common was however a very different threat to the locality, and the coming of the M4, slicing through the great estates of Englefield, Yattendon and Welford, changed Berkshire for good.

Brimpton had the good fortune to be on the western edge of the Wasing Estate, providing an oasis of rural life before the ever-growing conurbation of Thatcham and Newbury. The Mounts became very good friends and I was lucky enough to have a gun in the Wasing Syndicate for many years.

The Fairbanks had, as I have already explained, added a complete new wing on to the old Georgian mill house, the drawing-room of which was somewhat stark. I bought a complete room of William and Mary panelling from Angel, the Bath antique dealer, for a hundred and twenty pounds and got down to stripping it. I sent a small section to a furniture restorer in Shropshire we had got to know, who, having stripped it, gave me precise instructions how to proceed. It took me some nine months of hard toil as there were some fourteen coats of paint to be removed. A London-based carpenter (found by Lady Fairbank) then lived with us for several months while he installed it, very successfully.

A few years later Midgham House, on the other side of the Kennet valley, was being demolished and I bought all the panelling from what was known as the 'Duke's rooms'. In the early eighteenth century the house was owned by Stephen Poyntz, who became tutor to the young Duke of Cumberland, son of George II, and he added these rooms for his young charge. I stripped this panelling also but it took me far longer, not only because of a lot of intricate moulding which the earlier room did not have, but also because I was by then working during the week in London. This panelling went into the dining-room and next-door sitting-room.

To go back to 1951, we had an offer too good to refuse in October. Walter Rosen sent us first-class tickets on the *Queen Mary* to New York and an invitation to stay at Katonah, his extraordinary country house

William's wedding at Winchester, 1955. Olwen, the author,
Megan, Ruth and Bengy.

near Westchester, New York State, where he had put together a
remarkable collection of works of art, mainly from Italy. There was an
open-air theatre in the garden where Lucy Rosen (*née* Dodge) put on
summer concerts. My father was at that time living nearby, at Mount
Kisco, so we were able to see him and Anne several times.

Sadly, Walter suffered a stroke while we were staying and died while
we were on our way home on the *Queen Elizabeth*. We had seen, and
stayed with, other old friends of Ruth, especially Norman and Bobby
Woolworth, who were tremendously good fun and amazingly generous. As well as a sumptuous apartment on Fifth Avenue they had (and
daughter Pammie still has) a beautiful estate up in Maine, which was
run very much on English lines. In fact, Norman and Bobby were very
English orientated (Norman's father had owned the English Woolworths), had been married in London and were frequently over here.

They also had a butler called Sykes, who was Jeeves personified, and a Scots nanny for their children.

I have to confess that those two crossings in the old *Queens* spoilt me for ever; I was lucky enough to cross on them several more times later on, and the experience never palled. Once, in the 1960s we had been staying with the Woolworths in Maine and I brought the entire family back on the *Queen Elizabeth*; halfway across the Atlantic we passed the *Queen Mary* on her final crossing, closing to less than a thousand yards on a sunny afternoon.

The major event of 1952 was the arrival of my second son, Robert, on 13 August. He was born in my in-laws' house, 18 Thurloe Square, at two in the morning; he has always been called Robbie and has had a very interesting career which I shall go into later.

CHAPTER 13

The Coronation, 1953

Towards the end of 1952 I applied to be a gold-staff officer at the Coronation of Her Majesty Queen Elizabeth II, which was to take place the following June. In January I was appointed, along with several hundred others, and told to hold myself in readiness for rehearsals from 26 May onwards. We were mainly drawn from the armed forces (or retired members of same) with a fair preponderance of eldest sons of peers. It was certainly a fascinating experience and one I should have been sorry to have missed, since coronations don't come round all that often.

We had an initial briefing in the Central Methodist Hall, given by the chief gold-staff officer, Major-General R. G. Fielden, who explained our duties. These were mainly to get guests to their seats, generally nanny them for several hours and then get them out again. If this sounds easy, a glance at the plan of Westminster Abbey, with its medieval layout and curious corners, plus numerous doors, argues otherwise.

Eight of us were allocated to block AA3, which was situated at the first-tier level, in the north transept, looking straight down on to the theatre, so called because here was King Edward's Chair, where the actual crowning took place. In this block we were to have just over two hundred guests, comprising mainly privy counsellors who were not peers and their wives.

Most of us were thirtyish, such as Charlie Morpeth, later Earl of Carlisle, who had lost a leg with the Rifle Brigade in Italy and became a good friend of mine, but we had one much more senior figure in Cedric, Earl of Cardigan, who had done this chore before in 1937 and felt slightly put out that his elderly sire, Lord Ailesbury, was again to be in the family robes, while he was still a fifty-year-old gold stick.

Our block commander was a splendid Highlander, Brigadier Geoffrey McNab, who was at the time Military Attaché in Paris, and took the whole proceedings in a very relaxed and good-humoured manner.

Rehearsals went along pretty smoothly under the eagle eye of the Duke of Norfolk. As Earl Marshal he had officiated at King George VI's Coronation in 1937 when he was only twenty-nine, and there had been some criticism of the arrangements, especially in getting guests away after the ceremony. He was determined that this time there would be no hiccups, especially as the decision had been taken that the service would be televised.

At one rehearsal, the Archbishop of Canterbury, Dr Fisher, lost his place in the order of service and had to ask the Earl Marshal what happened next. 'You pray,' came the withering instruction from the leading Roman Catholic layman in the kingdom.

The final rehearsal was on 29 May when we all had to be in our places before 8 a.m., dressed as for the day itself, with a full complement of guests from the general public, and Lavinia, Duchess of Norfolk, standing in for the Queen. All went well until, just before the crowning ceremony, there was an almighty crash and one of the heralds, Sir Thomas Innes of Learney, Lyon King of Arms, fainted and hit the floor. Fortunately he was fully recovered by Coronation Day.

As I struggled into my velvet court dress, with white tie and black silk stockings, at 3.45 a.m. on the 2 June the day looked distinctly unpromising, with a cold wind and occasional bursts of squally rain. By 4.30 I was in Lowndes Street where I had arranged to collect my block commander, the gallant brigadier. He was an imposing sight, with several yards of plaid around his middle, an enormous headdress decorated with what appeared to be feathers from assorted protected species, a formidable sword *and* a shepherd's crook. Either one or both of these last-named items managed to wedge itself in the gate of the old-fashioned lift and there was a worrying moment when we saw ourselves stuck for some hours. Finally released, I put him in the back of the car and we arrived at Dean's Yard in good order.

Here an enormous marquee had been put up on the football ground belonging to Westminster School, and an excellent breakfast had been laid on. The variety of costume and uniform to be seen among some four hundred gold-staff officers was striking – I should think every regiment in the British army was represented.

A large annexe had been created outside the west door of the Abbey, where the various processions were to form up and where the Queen would in due course arrive. Passing through this we went straight to our allocated stations by 5.30, when watches had to be synchronised by Big Ben. All the doors of the Abbey were opened at six o'clock and closed at eight thirty. Although this sounds a reasonable time in which to seat some two thousand guests it was amazing how quickly it passed. Many found friends to gossip with on the way to their allotted seats and all were fascinated by the splendour of the scene before them.

Gone were the dust sheets that had covered the blue and gold hangings to the stalls and balconies during rehearsals, and gone too were the yards of cable for lighting and cameras that had coiled serpent-like everywhere. The covers to the seats and stools had been removed and now upon each, resplendent in dark blue with the royal cipher, was placed a finely bound order of service and a copy of the ceremonial so soon to be enacted. It all looked immaculate.

As each guest arrived we had tactfully to point out that after nine o'clock no one would be allowed to leave their seat to use the facilities provided; however they were all so busy greeting each other that there was quite an ugly rush just before the deadline.

We drew lots among the eight of us as to where we should be stationed and I was fortunate enough to find myself looking after the two rows nearest the balcony overlooking the theatre, which gave me a superb view once the proceedings started. Uncle Gwilym and Aunt Edna were among those in our front row. He was too tall to wear Taid's privy-council uniform, which was lent for the occasion to Harry Crookshank, the Lord Privy Seal (this uniform has, incidentally, now seen three coronations and sits in a glass case at my home).

Others I had in my charge were Herbert Morrison, Tom Johnston (later Secretary of State for Scotland), the Hore-Belishas, Sir Oliver and Lady Franks, and Mr and Mrs Clement Davies (he was then leader of the Liberal Party).

By looking over the balcony it was possible to see the peeresses, whose block was below us, and to compare tiaras. We gave first place to the Duchess of Portland, whose headdress was a stunning display of diamonds; several people commented on the modest adornments of the Duchess of Sutherland, who indeed had little apart from the coronet that she carried since burglars had ransacked her room a few hours previously. Fortunately one important item was safe: the diamond rivière necklace which had belonged to Mary Antoinette had been lent to the Duke's niece, Elizabeth Janson (now Countess of Sutherland).

I cannot now remember exactly the hour but it was during this waiting period that the thrilling news arrived, and was quickly passed from guest to guest, that Everest had at last been conquered. As the *Evening Standard*'s headline had it later in the day, this was the 'Crowning Glory'. Sadly today there seems to be an almost constant procession to the top of that fabled mountain.

Just before nine o'clock the processions from the annexe into the Abbey commenced. First were assorted minor royalties, including the Harewoods, Cambridges and Abel Smiths; then an immensely long line of foreign royals and representatives of foreign states, which included for instance Prince Bernhard of the Netherlands, General George Marshall for the USA and the Crown Prince of Japan. Queen Salote of Tonga was a very large lady and magnificently dressed. She had arrived in an open carriage which she shared with a diminutive and somewhat obscure little man. On being asked who he was, Noël Coward is reputed to have said, 'That is her lunch.'

Shortly after this the princes and princesses of the blood royal arrived and were led to the Royal Gallery, opposite us and slightly to the left. The Duke and Duchess of Gloucester, flanked by their two sons Princes William and Richard, the Duchess of Kent, looking quite lovely, and her three children, the elderly Athlones, immensely distinguished, and finally the venerable Princess Marie Louise.

There followed a separate procession of the Queen Mother and Princess Margaret, and the Royal Gallery was complete. The magnificent dresses and jewellery of every member of the royal family were wonderfully complemented by the tabards of the heralds who preceded them, and by their train bearers and personal members of their staff.

The procession of the Queen was of course the most magnificent of all, and immensely long and colourful. Led by the Abbey beadle, there followed the chaplains, representatives of the free churches and the cross of Westminster, closely followed by the dean, the Very Reverend Alan Don. Then a clutch of heralds, the officers of all the orders of knighthood, the standards of the Commonwealth countries, the Union Standard borne by Captain John Dymoke (who had not exercised his ancient right as Queen's Challenger to ride into Westminster Hall) and the Royal Standard borne by Field Marshal Montgomery.

The prime ministers of the Commonwealth were followed by Sir Winston Churchill, resplendent in the uniform of Warden of the Cinque Ports and garter robes and looking particularly pink and cherubic under the arc lights. Then came the Lord Chancellor (Lord Simonds), the Archbishop of Canterbury and the Duke of Edinburgh, flanked by gentlemen-at-arms, wonderfully theatrical in their plumed headdresses and carrying their axes.

The superb regalia, every piece of which was to play an integral role in the ceremony, came next, each item borne by a distinguished peer, and at last the Queen, in a robe of crimson velvet and a diadem of precious stones; she looked so young and vulnerable I think we all caught our breath at the thought of the long and complicated ritual ahead of her.

During this time the choir had been singing the hundred and twenty-second psalm, 'I was glad when they said unto me', and now the service proper began with the recognition, when the Archbishop went to the four sides of the theatre calling on people to acclaim their 'undoubted Queen', which they did lustily, shouting, 'God Save Queen Elizabeth.'

The Archbishop ministered the oath, the Bible was presented by the Moderator of the Church of Scotland and the communion service commenced, with the annointing being accompanied by that glorious anthem, 'Zadok the Priest'. We then witnessed the investing of the Queen with all the various items of the regalia; each had its ancient symbolism reflected in the prayers that accompanied it. For example, when the dean placed the armills (bracelets) upon the Queen's wrists he said:

> Receive the bracelets of sincerity and wisdom, both for tokens of the Lord's protection embracing you on every side; and also for symbols and pledges of that bond which unites you with your peoples . . .

and again when the Archbishop gave the rod with the dove to the Queen, he said:

> Receive the rod of equity and mercy. Be so merciful that you be not too remiss; so execute justice that you forget not mercy. Punish the wicked, protect and cherish the just, and lead your people in the way wherein they should go.

At last the great moment came when the Archbishop, having blessed St Edward's crown at the altar, brought it before the Queen and placed it on her head. All the princes and peers put on their coronets and the great cry went up, 'God save the Queen.' As the order of service (from which I have quoted) put it, 'and the trumpets shall sound, and by a signal given, the great guns at the Tower shall be shot off'. There was indeed a great deal of noise as the climax of the ceremony was reached and it was impossible to remain unmoved.

The homage followed, led by the Archbishop, and followed by Prince Philip who, kneeling before the Queen, said:

> I do become your liege man of life and limb, and of earthly worship: and faith and truth I will bear unto you, to live and die, against all manner of folks.

The senior peer of each degree then did homage, kneeling before the Queen, repeating the same oath and kissing her right hand. There were no tumbles, though some found it very testing to get up again in their heavy coronation robes and withdraw backwards.

After this the Queen moved back towards the altar and the communion service was completed, following which she went into St Edward's Chapel. Here she put on the imperial crown and, with the sceptre in one hand and the orb in the other, commenced her slow progress back down the choir and nave with the full National Anthem being sung, and thus passed out into the Broad Sanctuary where her golden coach awaited and where she was met by the tumultuous roars of her subjects.

What were our emotions at the close of this great occasion? Most of those present had played some part in that terrible war which had come to an end only eight years before, and the Coronation provided a unique opportunity for a reaffirmation of our historical strength and pride in our traditions. And there was also pride in ourselves that we had all, in however small a way, contributed to the success of such an immaculate ceremony. But I think above all it was a feeling of enormous admiration and affection for our lovely young Queen, who had been the focus of attention throughout this long ritual and who never once wavered.

Looking back at it after forty-five years – and I wonder today how many are still alive who had the privilege of being there – I cannot help reflecting how our present government would feel if the situation arose now. It is difficult to envisage New Labour feeling comfortable with such a display of old England, with so many of the leading roles being played by peers of the realm, when they are hell bent on their abolition and for constitutional change all round. One hopes that the question will not arise for many years to come.

This momentous day had an interesting conclusion. Jock Colville (then Churchill's private secretary) and his wife Meg were staying with us in Thurloe Square and managed to include Ruth and me in the small party that was to watch the fireworks that evening from the roof of the Air Ministry building.

The Prime Minister arrived after a very good dinner and in extremely good form, accompanied by his old friend El Glaoui, the Pasha of Marrakesh and Premier Lord of the Atlas (to give him his full titles). The latter, although a personal guest of Churchill, had been under the impression that he had been officially invited to the ceremony and in consequence brought with him, as a gift for the Queen, an emerald about the size of a pigeon's egg. This had thrown the Foreign Office into a terrible tizzy: to return it to the Glaoui would have been regarded as an outrageous insult, probably punishable by instant beheading. I never heard how the matter was resolved.

The fireworks were of course spectacular and Winston enjoyed them with schoolboy delight, waving his cigar in the air when a particularly fiery rocket exploded. 'That would cost you a very good dinner,' he would remark as a galaxy of coloured maroons filled the sky. El Glaoui, who spoke only French, remained unmoved when these and other jovial remarks were translated by Jock, and sat silently in his robes with a jewelled dagger at his side, his deep-set eyes quietly glistening. He was one of the most sinister men I have ever encountered.

When the performance was over we were all asked back to Downing Street for a drink; the ladies of the party were put into cars while Jock, Bill Deakin and I struggled on foot through the crowds that were milling about in Whitehall. The atmosphere at No. 10 was very much, 'Let's keep the party going.' Christopher and Mary Soames and the Nevills were in the small drawing-room when we arrived. Then Jock said the Prime Minister wanted to see me.

I went into the cabinet room where the old man was sitting in his accustomed chair, back to the fireplace, cigar going and looking at some papers. 'What will you have to drink?' he asked. I requested whisky and soda and the most enormous measure arrived. He asked me what I was doing, and why I wasn't in politics. I explained that I was farming in Berkshire and didn't seem to have time for anything else. 'Oh, you call it BURKshire, do you?' Jock (who had joined us) said, 'No, sir, he said BARKshire,' but Winston was determined to have his little joke. 'Oh well, my Welsh pronunciation isn't very good either,' followed by, 'I keep pigs too but I manage to keep my hand in at politics as well.'

After these pleasantries, he then reminisced at some length, and with great affection, about LG and his great abilities; 'He could always see into the next field,' he said. He kept returning to the question of why I wasn't in Parliament and finally said, 'Oh well, you will, the blood will out' (this last phrase with great relish). Jock finally indicated that I should take my leave as the old man was clearly tired – he had been up and dressed in his uniform as Lord Warden of the Cinque Ports in the

Abbey from an early hour and it was now after one the following morning.

In my fascination at our talk (or rather his talk) I had only drunk half of my whisky, which he noticed as I said good-night. 'You must not leave that, for the luck of the house, you know.' I drained it and left.

CHAPTER 14

Into Lloyd's

By 1954 it became abundantly clear that, however hard I worked, farming on such a small scale was never going to be very profitable. Added to which my father-in-law's business affairs took a distinct downturn; leaving the Biro pen company after a disagreement with his partner Harry Martin, he had bought an advertising agency which proved a costly error. Consequently he had to discontinue the generous allowance which he had made to Ruth on our marriage. And we had two small boys to bring up.

In November I therefore bought a new bowler hat and started work at Bland Welch & Company, at seven hundred pounds a year. This firm of Lloyd's insurance brokers had been established many years before; prior to the 1914–18 War it had handled the White Star Steamship account but fell down over the placing of the *Titanic* insurance (that ill-fated vessel being then the most expensive marine risk ever) and lost the business to rivals Willis Faber.

Now it was a rapidly growing firm under the dynamic leadership of Reggie Cheeseman, who had bought it during the war. In recent years a valuable link had been established with Marsh & McLennan, the leading American insurance brokers; in a curious way I had something to do with this, as I will explain.

When Walter Rosen came over for our wedding, Dicky Coit gave a lunch at the Savoy for him, to which Wilfrid Janson was invited. Wilfrid asked if he might bring his friend Reggie Cheesman; the latter made a deep impression on Walter, who, on his return to New York sent for Lawrence Kennedy, then president of Marsh & McLennan. Walter's bank, Ladenberg Thalmann, provided financial backing to Marsh and

Mr Kennedy willingly accepted Walter's suggestion that a trading relationship should be established with Bland Welch.

Lloyd's in those far-off days was still in the 1928 building, situated between Leadenhall Street and Lime Street, with an extension into the Royal Mail building next door. The underwriting room was neo-classical in design, heavily columned, and with four dramatic and colourful paintings on the ceiling with allegorical figures depicting scenarios such as 'Commerce rewarding the Fruits of Industry.'

These high-flown sentiments were to a limited extent reflected in the scene below, where the underwriters sat in the same boxes that they had had in the Royal Exchange, some still wore silk top hats, and there was a definite air that the trade being carried on was a gentlemanly one, and not in any sense to be confused with what went on down the road in the Stock Exchange. The somewhat Dickensian atmosphere was heightened during the winter months when a good old-fashioned pea-souper fog drifted in from the street, making it quite difficult to see across the room.

For those unfamiliar with how Lloyd's works I should explain that the underwriter sitting in his box is responsible for the profit or loss of all the 'names' who may be members of his syndicate, the majority of whom will be 'external' names; these will have satisfied the authorities that they have a sufficient level of wealth and will have made a substantial deposit into Lloyd's. Thus when he is presented with a 'slip' by a broker and invited to write a 'line', be it a ship, aircraft or ice-cream factory, the underwriter is accepting a share not only for himself but for each and every member of his syndicate.

To illustrate this further and take a famous example, the *Titanic* slip,* taken into the market by Willis Faber & Dumas in January 1912 for a total value of a million pounds (an unprecedented sum in those days), carried a rate of only fifteen shillings per cent (reflecting the 'unsinkable' label attached to the unhappy vessel), and many underwriters cheerfully wrote lines of twenty and thirty thousand pounds, all of which they and their names subsequently lost.

Business can come to the underwriters only through Lloyd's brokers,

* C. Wright & C. E. Fayle, *History of Lloyd's*

who receive their instructions from their clients. It is the broker's duty to place the risk at the most advantageous rate, at the same time making a full disclosure to the underwriter of all material facts. It has always seemed to me that the art of successful broking lay in presenting the risk in as attractive a light as possible without covering up any serious deficiencies.

I had an unhappy experience early on in my career at Lloyd's when I had to place a 'voyage' insurance on a particular vessel that was engaged in a complicated journey in northern waters, including, I think, Hudson's Bay. I had made quite good progress and completed nearly half of my slip when I approached a distinguished and some-what elderly gentleman at his box one day after lunch. I unfolded my story, leaving out no detail of the proposed odyssey, and anxiously awaited a question or two, or at least some comment. None came, and I attempted to reinforce the essential elements of the risk. Still nothing was said. At last another broker, queueing behind me, whispered, 'I think you've sent him to sleep.' It was only too true and for a moment I thought I had better return to farming.

But there was a lot of camaraderie in the Room and one rapidly made a lot of friends. Quite a few underwriters had served in the war in the Brigade of Guards, so it never hurt to be seen wearing a Brigade tie. The masonic element at Lloyd's was also very strong (not that I was ever a mason), and close ties were also forged between members of the various societies – yachting, golf, dramatics and so forth.

The place abounded in characters. Charlie Hewitt, who had a very small syndicate but made a fortune for himself and his names by specialising in personal-effects insurance, for which he invariably charged '£5 in full', quite regardless of value. When he had to move from the Royal Exchange in 1928 one of his clerks found forty thousand pounds in bearer bonds at the back of a drawer. In 1965, a replica of the *Mayflower* was built to sail to America three hundred and fifty years on, and the slip to cover her voyage was very much a prestige document in which every syndicate was asked to participate. On being shown it, Charlie, then well into his nineties, astonished the broker by asking, 'Is this a renewal to me?'

Then there was Toby Green, underwriter for the Percy Janson (PJ) syndicate, started early in the nineteenth century. Toby was a very shrewd underwriter who made substantial profits for his names, but was something of a buccaneer, with an ill-concealed contempt for the committee of Lloyd's, which he steadfastly refused to join. To me he represented the best type of underwriter; show him something new, something unusual that could not easily be covered by a standard policy form and his interest was aroused. He was a genuine innovator, and that has always been one of Lloyd's strengths.

Another innovator, some would prefer to say a maverick, a few years later, was Ian Posgate, known cheerfully in the market as 'Goldfinger'. He single-handedly pioneered 'kidnap and ransom' insurance and related political risks and he too made consistently good returns for his names. Unusually, if he liked a risk, he would take it a hundred per cent for himself, which was considered by other underwriters to be rather ungentlemanly. He also regularly wrote annually more than his total premium income (calculated by the aggregate 'line' of all the members of his syndicate) and incurred the ire of the committee on many occasions. His most serious misjudgement, however, lay in the choice of his business associates, which was his undoing.

Reggie Cheeseman was a broker *par excellence*, who had gone straight into Lloyd's from school at fifteen and learnt the business the hard way and with no help other than his innate talent and capacity for hard work. His handling of underwriters was masterly and a joy to listen to; quite softly spoken, he would say, 'I've got something really special for you here, old son,' and so compelling was his charm and persuasiveness that the pen was in the underwriter's hand within minutes.

He had a particular rapport with Toby Green, who 'led' many of our pioneering placements in the 1950s, such as 'all-in' policies for large American utility companies, and the first master policy for drilling rigs in the Gulf of Mexico. When the era of super-tankers arrived, Reggie wrested a substantial share of both the Niarchos and Onassis fleets from other brokers. He also made a large impact in the market by placing 'first-loss' policies, whereby instead of a client having to insure every penny of his operations, a calculation would be made of what was the possible maximum loss he could sustain; the savings in premium were of course dramatic.

Our offices were in a building in Fenchurch Street; here in a large room on the second floor the directors of Bland Welch sat at an enormous table, the way in which I believe old-fashioned merchant bankers used to operate; the advantage was that they could communicate easily with each other at all times, and with Reggie who sat just inside the door. We lesser mortals perched on the perimeter of the magic circle, preparing slips or 'devilling' for a director. Hours were long and often unpredictable, especially on the American side of the business because of the time lag, and one was frequently still in the office at eight or nine at night. Lloyd's was also open for business on Saturday mornings in those days, though mercifully I managed to avoid too many of those.

There were only about three hundred people in Bland Welch at that time and one rapidly got to know most of them; among the thirty or so who were actually broking (for which one had a 'substitute' ticket for the Room) were some interesting individuals. Bill George had been a merchant seaman in the war, torpedoed twice, and had an irrepressible sense of the ridiculous as well as an endless repertoire of stories, all of which enhanced his broking ability. Don Coombe, an engaging Londoner, also had the gift of the gab in ample measure; he started a scheme for giving poor East End boys an annual holiday in the Channel Islands, sacrificing his own hard-earned holiday to run this fortnightly event. This in due course developed into a registered charity, widely supported by the whole Lloyd's community, and extended to include a retirement home for the elderly, thus providing for old as well as young. It flourishes today under Don's paternal eye and he has recently received a very well-merited MBE for all these great endeavours. We also had with us Nim Hall, who had played full back for England on many occasions; a modest, immensely likeable person, he never really developed in the firm and drifted out of sight. Then there was John Stanley, who had won a Military Cross in Crete during the war, and was one of the four who were incarcerated in Cairo by President Nasser. Together with his delightful wife Lily, who was a talented opera singer, we had some very jolly evenings, and John and I developed a lot of business for the firm in Glasgow among other places.

On the whole, Lloyd's was a very interesting place to be in and the life of a broker was rarely dull; our firm, under Reggie's leadership, was at an exciting moment of rapid expansion, and the momentum carried one along. At the same time there was a recognised code of conduct, both for brokers and underwriters; the senior figures in Lloyd's such as Guy Chester (a leading Methodist incidentally) and Roy Merritt were regarded with some awe and held in great respect. David Bradstock was one day showing a risk to the great Sir Eustace Pulbrook, then in his third term as chairman of Lloyd's; the risk duly written, David (ever a keen racegoer) ventured to suggest that a certain horse in the 2.30 at Kempton was a sure-fire winner. Sir Eustace's moustaches quivered with shock, and after David's hurried departure, rang up his boss and complained of what he considered very ungentlemanly conduct in a broker. David was duly told to go and apologise to the great man, and in doing so managed to get in that the horse in question had actually won. 'I know,' said Sir Eustace, 'I had five pounds each way on it.'

But one did not in a general way take liberties with these gentlemen, and Lloyd's motto, *Fidentia*, was adhered to in all our commerce. Scandals were unheard of; these came later, and were almost exclusively the result of greed. In the 1960s and 1970s the overall premium income of Lloyd's grew rapidly, as did the number of underwriting members. When I was elected a member in 1959, there were about six thousand, of whom some two thousand were 'working names' like myself, and the remainder 'outside' names, who rarely came to see their underwriting agent and were content to receive an annual cheque. By 1970, the total was twenty thousand plus and it eventually peaked at thirty-four thousand in 1989. Unfortunately, a great many of these new 'outside' names had been recruited by unscrupulous agents; many had little more than the value of their house as collateral and were certainly not in a position to write out a six-figure cheque, as many were asked to do in due course. Today (1998), as I write, the number of underwriting names has shrunk to the six thousand that existed forty years ago, and a great tidal wave of disaster has swept over many of the other unfortunates. But that is another story that I do not propose to recount now.

In the summer of 1956 Reggie Cheeseman asked me to go to America to work for a few months in Marsh & McLennan's head office in Chicago, taking Ruth with me. It was made clear to me that the object was not just for me to gain experience with this leading US broker but also to get to know as many as possible of the key individuals there, and generally to build bridges. It was an exciting assignment.

We left the boys (both of whom had started at Wagner's Pre-Prep School) in the tender care of Ruth's parents at Thurloe Square, the farm being looked after by Wendy Hilliard, my diminutive but resourceful manager, and set sail for New York on the *Queen Mary* in late August. Fellow passengers included Rachel and William Douglas-Home, the latter on his way to Hollywood to oversee the filming of his *Reluctant Débutante*, and a very lively travelling companion he was too. On arrival we had barely time to drop our luggage at the St Regis Hotel before Pammie Woolworth took us off to see *My Fair Lady*, then playing to packed houses at the Mark Hellinger Theatre – a wonderful way to arrive in New York.

After a brief visit to Toronto, where we had an office, we went by train to Chicago and were put up temporarily at the Racquet Club before moving into an apartment hotel, the Park Dearborn. From here I would take the tram downtown every morning to Marsh's office on South La Salle Street.

Hermon D. Smith (always known as 'Dutch') was then president of the firm and gave me a warm welcome before passing me on to Howard Gillette, who looked after me for the first few weeks. He and his wife Mary were particularly kind and introduced us to many of their Chicago friends. I spent time in almost every part of the office, went out on visits to clients, sat in on some fascinating presentations of 'risk assessment' and met a varied and illuminating cross-section of the insurance industry. Marsh's clients covered every type of industry from airlines, the big utilities and leading manufacturers to ships and oil rigs. The latter were the special province of Al Morey, a colourful character with whom I spent a lot of time and whom I admired a lot.

Soon after I arrived the eminent architect, Frank Lloyd Wright, gave a presentation in the Palmer House Hotel of his proposed 'mile high' skyscraper: its five hundred floors were to be reached by multiple lifts operating like vertical trains serving ten floors simultaneously and driven by nuclear power. By this arrangement the building could be evacuated, so he claimed, in twenty minutes. The foundations were to be designed with the giant redwood tree in mind, which has an immensely strong and deep tap root; Wright's 'tap root' would be of reinforced concrete and would allow the top of the five-thousand-foot building to sway some twenty feet in the winds that habitually swept off Lake Michigan. I found it absolutely fascinating but was not totally surprised when the Chicago planners turned the scheme down.

The other great event at the Palmer House Hotel that autumn was the Democratic Convention, with all the razzmatazz that these occasions generate. Adlai Stevenson, who was the Democratic choice to run against Eisenhower, had a fervent supporter in 'Dutch' Smith and his family; we all went to the theatre together on one occasion and I was intrigued by the shape of Stevenson's head – he was a classic 'egghead'. He was of course unsuccessful in his bid for power.

In October the Suez Crisis erupted. I had omitted to notify the War Office that I had gone to America (as an officer on the emergency reserve this was then obligatory) and had to send a hasty cable to Jerry Spencer-Smith. But what was rather more serious, as that dreadful week unfolded, was coming into the office as the only Briton and realising the really deep resentment our extraordinary actions had engendered, of all places in what was traditionally the heart of isolationism, by Eden not even picking up the telephone to tell the President what we were up to. I think Anglo-American relations hit an all-time low.

I became very fond of Chicago and made a lot of good friends; everyone was so hospitable and kind. Some of the finest houses are at Lake Forest, north of the city, looking on to Lake Michigan, and the Blossom family owned one of these. Mr George Blossom was president of Fred S. James, another Chicago insurance broking house with whom we corresponded, and I spent some time in their office also. His son, George W. Blossom III, always known as Bud, has now been a firm friend for more than forty years.

Don McLennan, grandson of the eponymous firm's founder, also had a splendid house at Lake Forest; staying there one weekend I disgraced myself by passing out during dinner. I had indeed consumed several Martinis, and Chicago measures were always generous, but I was none the less mystified (since I have a fairly strong head) until Don confessed that the Martinis were from a jug left in the fridge from a previous party. This apparently can render them almost lethal in their potency.

I wrote a weekly letter (typed by Ruth) to Reg in which I reported progress, and he replied from time to time with suggestions that I should make a special effort to meet so-and-so which I duly did. In November I got a cable from Mike Adams to say that we had landed the McAlpine business. A year previously I had written to Uncle Malcolm asking if we might have the opportunity to put forward our ideas, and this was the result. It gave a great lift to my spirits and was to have a marked impact on my subsequent career at Lloyd's.

By early December my tour of duty was over and, after a short spell in Marsh's New York office, we sailed for home in the *Queen Elizabeth*. Halfway across the Atlantic we received bad news: my mother-in-law, Violet, had died very suddenly. She was a wonderful woman in every way, and had become a very loving grandmother to our two little boys; so this was a sad homecoming indeed, after what had otherwise been a fascinating and successful visit.

CHAPTER 15

Deaths and Entrances

I look back at the 1960s as a time of mixed fortune: a growing family, my star rising in the business world – then a succession of deaths among my closest relatives.

Julia, our third child, had been born in 1958, proving a model child from the start and a great joy to us all ever since. In 1959 David went to Heatherdown; the headmaster, Charles Warner, died suddenly soon after, and was succeeded by James Edwards, whose grandfather, the Bishop of St Asaph, had been a friend of LG. Robbie joined David at Heatherdown in 1960 and the regular pattern of school outings, fathers' matches and holidays became part of life.

In 1960 Reggie Cheeseman died very suddenly, aged fifty-six, and there was an immediate hiatus at Bland Welch. A year or two before his death he had sold twenty-five per cent of the firm to Samuel Montagu the merchant banker, who had an option to buy any other slice of the business that became available. With a substantial death-duty bill to be paid on Reggie's death, Samuel Montagu (subsequently to become part of Midland Bank) assumed control and put in an ex-director of the Bank of India, Peter Beale, as chairman.

I did not find the new arrangement to my liking and in 1962 accepted an offer from George Stephens to become a director of the firm he had just created by merging his own firm with that of Lord Poole's, Thomas Stephens Poole. Here I found some very congenial companions, including Ronnie Kershaw, already a friend and neighbour in the country, Geoffrey Merton and Eamon Fitzgerald.

Eamon had had a distinguished career during the war, winning a Military Cross with the Guards Armoured Division (as had Geoffrey

Merton) and later married Julie, a daughter of that unit's commander, Sir Allan Adair. After a spell in the Crown Office in Kenya, Eamon came to Lloyd's. Here he specialised in arranging complicated family tax-avoidance schemes, at which he was expert. He was a very gregarious person, extremely funny and very kind, especially to other people's children. He was a firm believer in the long lunch, and when lunching with him it was unusual to get back to the City before three o'clock. I gather that things are very different nowadays.

Thomas Stephens Poole came to an untimely end around 1968; they had a controlling interest in the St Helen's Insurance Company which went under as a direct result of the 1964 hurricane season. Thomas Stephens Poole were left in a precarious situation and were absorbed into Bain Dawes.

In the meantime there had been changes at Bland Welch: they had merged with E.W. Payne, becoming Bland Payne, and Neil Mills had become chairman. Neil had been one of Reggie's original bright young men and a director from the early days; we had always been good friends and he now asked me to return.

During my years at Thomas Stephens Poole I had never attempted to move the very substantial brokerage account which I had built up, in fact under an agreement between the two firms the brokerage was shared. I now therefore proposed to Neil that if I returned I should be allowed to form my own company, as well as becoming a director of Bland Payne, and this is what happened. In due course I sold the business back to the firm, in three stages, enabling me to make a modest amount of capital.

Early in the 1960s I was elected to White's, one of the happiest events of my life and one for which I was indebted to my proposer, Fred Cripps. The Cripps family were cousins of my mother-in-law; at the time of our marriage Stafford Cripps, the youngest of four brothers, was Chancellor of the Exchequer, generally known at the time as 'Austerity Cripps'. There was nothing austere about brother Fred, however. A *bon vivant par excellence*, he was a flamboyant personality, always beautifully dressed, with bow tie and monocle and, in cold weather, a flowing cloak in which he both shot and fished. Born in 1885, he had been at New College when the warden was the eccentric Dr Spooner, about whom he had a good stock of stories; later, in the 1914–18 War he commanded the Royal Bucks Yeomanry, winning two DSOs and the Belgium Croix de Guerre.

Before that war he ran (not very successfully) a bank in Russia, where he had numerous adventures, including an encounter with Rasputin. He also met and became firm friends with the great Russian bass, Feodor Chaliapin, whom he first encountered on a train journey between Moscow and St Petersburg, during which (so Fred's story went) they consumed an entire case of champagne.

Some years later, 1921 to be precise, Chaliapin was in London and my grandfather wished to meet him. This was duly arranged at a lunch at the Carlton Hotel with Fred acting as interpreter (for Chaliapin spoke no English). The conversation went something like this:

LG (to Fred): 'Would you ask him how long he thinks the present government will last?'
(Fred interprets)
Chaliapin: 'Tell him I don't know anything about politics, I am a singer, but I do like champagne and my glass is empty.'
Fred (to LG): 'He says it is very hard to say.' (The bottle is passed.)
LG (to Fred): 'Ask him what sort of harvest they have in Russia.'
Chaliapin: 'Good God, I'm not a farmer – pass me more champagne!'

and so lunch proceeded. At the end LG said to Fred, 'What a diplomat your friend is!'

Fred had been married to Violet Nelson, later Duchess of Westminster, but by the time I got to know him they were divorced and he was living happily near Newbury, looked after by an old friend from his youth. Later, he had to move into a nursing home; while there he succeeded his elder brother, Seddon, as Lord Parmoor, but sadly was never fit enough to attend the House of Lords, which he would have much enjoyed and where he would have received a great welcome from his many friends there.

Winston Churchill died in January 1965, and his elaborate state funeral took place a few days later, following a three-day lying-in-state in Westminster Hall. The Welsh Office was then in Gwydir House,

Whitehall, and Goronwy, by then Permanent Under-Secretary for Wales, suggested we might like to view the procession from his splendid first-floor office. I took Julia, then aged six, keen for her to be able to say in later years that she had witnessed the great man going to his last rest. It was a bitterly cold day and the crowds watched silently as, to a muffled drumbeat, the coffin on its gun-carriage was pulled by a contingent of sailors. I could not but reflect on the contrast with that other funeral, twenty years earlier, when LG, Churchill's lifelong friend, had been laid to rest with such simplicity at Llanystumdwy. As the procession drew level with our viewing point, with the Duke of Norfolk marching steadily in front of the bier, a piping voice rang out from Julia, 'Daddy, what's in that box?'

To return to family matters, my mother and Uncle David had had a series of house moves; after Owlswood was sold in 1951 (the garden became too much and the water supply was erratic), they moved to Lowder Mill, an attractive property also near Haslemere with a lake. Then Uncle David took silk and within a year or two was appointed county-court judge for the mid-Wales circuit. They rented several houses before buying Plas Gwyn, at Aberedw, near Builth Wells. Here they settled happily, with David fully enjoying his new role (which included being chairman of the local Quarter Sessions) and my mother contented with a small and manageable garden and the challenge of the short stretch of the Wye which went with the house. Every winter she took off for the sun, generally by boat, to South America, Spain or Madeira, David going along if he could fit it in between court sittings.

Disaster struck one day in September 1961 when David, having had a very long and liquid lunch, was involved in a minor traffic accident. All would have been well had he not been very aggressive to those who were trying to assist; the police were called, the usual tests taken (this was long before the breathalyser) and he was found guilty of being under the influence. The then Lord Chancellor, Lord Kilmuir (David Maxwell-Fyfe as was – nicknamed in Wales 'Dai Bananas'), was not prepared to overlook the matter and David had to resign as a judge, I believe the first ever to be compromised in this way. It was a bitter blow and put a great strain on both of them, my mother not having been well at the time.

The author's mother

During the following year David tried, unsuccessfully, to be re-appointed to the bench, and eventually accepted a position as a member of the Foreign Compensation Commission. This, of course, involved staying all week at his club, with my mother alone in Radnorshire, although she continued to go abroad every winter.

In 1966 she had gone to South Africa on an Ellerman ship, *City of Pretoria*, and was on her way home when she contracted pneumonia and died at sea on 10 March. I was in New York on a business trip when this shocking news came through. David was in hospital recovering from an eye operation; my mother's body was put ashore at Dakar, West Africa, and it was not until May that we were able to bury her, according to her wishes, up on the hillside above Plas Gwyn.

Within a few days I was heading for Criccieth for Aunt Megan's funeral. She had developed lung cancer the previous year but fought it valiantly, though she was too ill to contest the 1966 election. Gwilym Prys Davies addressed meetings in Carmarthenshire on her behalf, ably assisted by Benjy, and, *in absentia*, she achieved the highest majority since she had won the seat for Labour in 1957. I saw her last when she was in Hammersmith hospital in January, and then she made a brave attempt to make light of her condition. She was, like her father, a 'bonny fichter'.

There can be little doubt that had Hugh Gaitskell become Prime Minister, Megan, who was a close friend and of similar political sympathies, would have achieved cabinet office. I was staying with her at Brynawelon when Gaitskell died so suddenly and her distress was palpable. 'Oh, Lord,' she said, 'now we shall have Harold Wilson.' At the end of her life, when she was really too ill to appreciate it, she was made a Companion of Honour.

Uncle Gwilym died the following year, 1967, having gone to the Lords as Viscount Tenby a decade earlier. He had had the unenviable task of trying to help my father financially from the 'LG Fund', such as it was, after he returned from the USA and at the same time passed on to me certain family memorabilia which had miraculously escaped Frances's clutches. We met fairly frequently, sometimes for lunch and now and again in the McAlpine 'box' at Epsom; he was always the same,

His Honour D. Eifion Evans QC (Uncle David)

full of fun and jokes, and I shall always think of him with great affection.

I have already described the ups and downs of my father's sojourn in the USA from 1947 to 1958. After his return he went to stay at Criccieth with Aunt Olwen, where he was very happy and seemed to be recovering his old form. We had let Brimpton for a year to Lord Norrie but I went every weekend to the cottage and my father came there for a few weeks, happily pottering about. But from things that he said I sensed that he still harboured a grudge against Taid, and indeed the rest of the family, on the grounds that he had been disinherited. In view of the fact that everyone was doing their utmost to support him financially, this was an unfortunate attitude to take, to say the least.

Sure enough, in 1959, he leapt into print with three lengthy interviews in the *Sunday Dispatch*, in which he took fairly broad swipes at everybody, but particularly Taid, and in a secondary role, Frances. As he had by then moved into one of Megan's cottages on the estate at Churt, near to where Frances lived at Avalon, this hardly made for good neighbourly relations.

He then announced that he was writing a book, entitled simply *Lloyd George*. As this was clearly to be very much his version of family life with his father and an amplification of the Sunday articles, there was a good deal of unease among the family. Valerie and I were eventually able to obtain a proof copy of the book from the publishers, Frederick Muller & Company, and it was submitted for Counsel's opinion. This stated, quite correctly, that 'the Law did not recognise that libels on a deceased person can inflict on surviving relations any damage sufficient to sustain an action unless their own reputations are also impugned.'

At the end of his Advice, Colin Duncan QC said:

So much for the Law, with which I am really alone concerned; but if I may, for a moment, go beyond my instructions, I should hazard the guess that very little harm will be done, for example, to LG's great grandsons at school. The old man is already almost legendary (like Queen Victoria and King Edward VII) and I can hardly imagine his supposed frailties will really matter much to the contempories of his great grandchildren.

Forty years on I acknowledge the wisdom of this observation. Even though every current political scandal has the tabloids frantically dredging their memories of what LG did or was supposed to have done in his day, I have yet to learn of any of my children, or indeed grandchildren, suffering any special trauma as a result.

On the other hand I do encounter from time to time a lot of ignorance about LG, who by now might fairly be accepted as an historical figure. A year or so ago I was asked by HTV Bristol to contribute to a programme on my grandfather; on their way to interview me at home the two producers called in at Cardiff University and asked some of the students what they knew about Lloyd George. The immediate reply was, 'Oh, he was that naughty old man, wasn't he?'

A year after his book was published my father entered the lists again, this time as a playwright. Although I never saw the play, and it only appeared locally, at the tiny Castle Theatre, Farnham, he obviously had a lot of fun with it. With the title *Storm Lantern*, the play has LG thinly disguised as the principal character, Morgan, and two characters called Brewster and Crump recognisable as Kitchener and Haig. In addition, there is a pretty suffragette, in whom Morgan becomes interested, and who was certainly supposed to be Frances. The Dowager Countess evidently consulted her solicitors but as the play was clearly not going to sweep the West End the matter was dropped.

It is no good pretending that my father's last years were happy ones. Although Anne came back from America and resumed her devoted care of him, years of over-indulgence took their toll on mind and body and he was moved into hospital. Here he died, from pneumonia, on 1 May 1968, in his eightieth year. And so the family vault in Criccieth cemetery was opened for the third time in less than two years. High above the town and with a splendid view of the castle and Cardigan Bay, it is within a few hundred yards of his birthplace, Mynydd Ednyfed.

One immediate effect of my father's death was that on becoming a peer I was no longer eligible to hold the office of high sheriff for Berkshire, for which I had been nominated by Teddy Goschen and which I was due to take up in 1971. Teddy said that as it would have been up to me to suggest a successor, in the normal course of events, I had better find a substitute. I duly gave Michael Webster, an old friend and fellow-gun on the Wasing shoot, a good lunch before apprising him of my request; he responded nobly and was a very popular and conscientious high sheriff, in spite of the fact that during his year of office he, as chairman of Watney, Combe, Reid, was fighting off a hostile takeover bid from Charles Clore. I was sorry, none the less, that events prevented me from carrying out this duty since it would have been a way of repaying something of what I owe to the county of my adoption.

I duly took my seat in the Lords in July; I had decided to sit on the cross-benches since I did not anticipate being able to take part in debates regularly and it seemed rather bogus to take a party whip if you were not able to attend and in any event I did not, nor do I now, regard myself as a political animal. Lord Strang (who had been permanent secretary at the Foreign Office) was then the convenor of the independent peers and gave me a kindly welcome.

The Leader of the House was Lord Shackleton and Lord Salisbury was leader of the Conservative opposition; wartime figures, such as Alexander and Montgomery, were regular attenders, while the cross-benches included such diverse figures as the venerable Lord Salter and Bob Boothby. So it was with a good deal of trepidation that I rose to my feet in May 1969 to make my maiden speech, in a debate on Welsh affairs; needless to say I was, as is customary, treated with great kindness and generous praise – quite undeserved. I managed to get in a mention of the fact that, prior to his investiture, the Prince of Wales was doing a course in the Welsh language at Aberystwyth where, as I put it, he had endeared himself to all, both 'town and gown'.

I was shortly to be involved in this interesting ceremony, which I feel deserves a chapter to itself.

CHAPTER 16

The Investiture, 1969

Until 1911 the ceremony of the Investiture of the Prince of Wales had been in abeyance for three hundred years, since Prince Henry in 1610 and Prince Charles (later Charles II) in 1616 had been invested, and considerable research by the then Earl Marshal was required to follow the precedents of those earlier occasions.

In 1908 Taid had been appointed Constable of Caernarvon Castle and this inspired him to press for the revival of the Investiture ceremony (though I believe it was actually suggested to him by his friend Dr Edwards, Bishop of St Asaph). He envisaged it as symbolising the national entity of Wales, and emphasising the distinctive characteristics of the Welsh nation. His suggestion received ready support in royal circles and the occasion was generally acclaimed as a spectacular success, being, for the first time in six hundred years, a public ceremony. That earlier public occasion was the presentation to the Welsh people of his infant son by Edward I in 1284; the baby had been born in the castle and Edward had craftily promised a child who could not speak a word of English – nor for that matter any other tongue.

So in 1969 there was a ready blueprint of what was required, and the Earl Marshal put the machinery in motion. He wrote to me in November 1968 saying the 'he had it in command from Her Majesty the Queen to invite me to take part in the Ceremony . . . ' I was subsequently told that my duties would be to carry the sword. There were five of us carrying the regalia and the other four were: Lord Ogmore, former president of the Welsh Liberals, Lord Heycock, former chairman of the Glamorgan County Council, Lord Maelor, former MP for Merioneth, and Lord Harlech, who as David Ormsby-Gore had been our ambassador in Washington. Sad to relate I now find myself the only survivor of these five.

We had a series of rehearsals in London, some at Buckingham Palace and others in St James Palace. In the former the rough shape of the castle and our route through it was laid out in white tape on the lawn; unfortunately it was impossible to reproduce the frequent steps up and down, typical of a medieval fortress, so it looked a little too easy.

In St James's Palace we practised handing the regalia to the Queen (or rather her stand-in). In my case the sword was borne on a cushion and I became concerned that there would be no means by which the Queen could know which end of the belt to accept (the sword was to be worn 'bendwise' by the prince, i.e. slung over the shoulder). I therefore suggested to Eric Penn, one day in White's, that we should dispense with the cushion; I could then offer the sword right way round and all would be well. This was accepted.

As the day approached there was a certain feeling of unease as to how the ceremony was going to be received in Wales. The so-called Free Wales Army had been making a nuisance of themselves in various ways and a number of student bodies in the University of Wales were obviously opposed; this did not deter Prince Charles, who was working through a crash course in the Welsh language at Aberystwyth. Some said that the best one could hope for was a silent crowd, or even one turning its back on the processions. I certainly made a diary note at the time that I had been told on very good authority that the Duke of Norfolk was adamant that if he was convinced of a serious threat of trouble, even with as little as a week to go before the event, he would recommend abandoning it altogether.

The Earl Marshal made his headquarters at Vaynol, home of Michael Duff, and very handy for Caernarvon. Jerry Spencer-Smith, now a major-general and commanding troops in Wales, stayed there also, as did many others, to enjoy Michael's generous hospitality. Antony Armstrong-Jones, now Lord Snowdon, had become Constable of Caernarvon Castle, and was very busy designing the layout for the ceremony inside the castle walls. Relations between him and Bernard

Norfolk were not exactly cordial. A few days before the final rehearsal Snowdon, who of course lived nearby, and a few friends had been in a launch on the Menai Straits when they had inadvertently come under fire from the cannons at Fort Belan, owned by Lord Newborough. That evening at dinner at Vaynol a young staff officer was recounting the incident to the Duke: 'And do you know, sir, one of Lord Newborough's cannon balls only just missed Lord Snowdon.' 'What a pity,' was the icy comment.

Goronwy, as Permanent Under-Secretary at the Welsh Office, also played a leading role in the planning of the ceremony, for which he subsequently received a well-earned knighthood.

The final rehearsal (in plain clothes) on 30 June was not a total success; several of the processions were coming in several minutes late, notably one containing all the Welsh MPs who were so busy gossiping that they forgot what they were supposed to be doing. A general rocket was delivered by the Earl Marshal, with an earnest plea for everyone to do better on the morrow.

I made a diary entry after the Investiture and I do not think I can do better than quote it in full:

1 July 1969. Robbie was up at 4.30 a.m. at Mrs Padmore's and off to Caernarvon by car, with two very attractive girls, to get a good position; he subsequently stood near the King's Gate and saw everything outside the Castle – arrivals, departures, disturbances, etc.

We dressed at leisure and left Eisteddfa about 10.30 after hurried photographs in a fine drizzle. Jeremy Thorpe in morning coat, very disappointed that other Privy Counsellors would not wear uniform, Heath particularly adamant it would seem. My Welsh Guards tunic, overalls and spurs much admired by the girls and Benjy's children.

By Pen-y-groes the cloud had begun to lift somewhat and at Caernarvon the sun was out as we left the car park and walked across the River Seiont to the Castle. I left the ladies outside the King's Gate, which they entered to reach their seats in the upper ward, and went to the Council offices. Here we each had a small and rather dingy room according to which procession we were in. Our little party comprised

Ogmore, Maelor, Heycock, Harlech, Davies,* Dynevor† and myself. Sandwiches were produced out of paper bags and for an hour or so we gossiped, wandered into other rooms to find friends, or looked out of the window at the crowds still arriving, and speculated on the weather.

At last a marshal came in and said, 'Fifteen minutes to go,' and we were then robed by a man from Ede & Ravenscroft. (I was at that time without my own and had borrowed from Eileen Bissill the robe that had belonged to her cousin Roger, last Earl of Stamford). Mine appeared to be of greater antiquity than the others; by contrast, Llew Heycock told us with great pride how his colleagues in Glamorgan had got together and raised £300 to buy him a robe. Alas, it looked terrible, not even good rabbit but a sort of foamy plastic substance, definitely ersatz ermine. I had to borrow a handkerchief from David Ogmore, my cold was still troubling me.

Out we go, up the street in loose formation, into a sort of parking lot, where we get into our proper order, thus:

Lord Aberdare   Earl of Plymouth   Lord Morris of Borth-y-gest
Sir Ben Bowen Thomas   Sir Hugo Boothby†
Sir Walkin Williams-Wynn§   George Thomas¶   LG
Lord Ogmore   Lord Heycock   Lord Maelor   Lord Harlech

At 1.20 p.m. we are over the start line; memories of similar movement orders twenty-five years ago on wet Italian slopes, but at least now there are some people to cheer us on, and so far, thank God, we have not been fired on! We go slowly up Shire Hall Street and get a good clap. I see Robbie two yards away, looking incredulously at his father in his finery – I don't know whether he is proud or embarrassed, anyway I give him a wink and on we go. The streets are now packed and there is an air of real excitement and buzz as we go down under the arch and swing left to the Water Gate. Up the steps (where a poor old lady, a guest, arriving two hours earlier had slipped and broken her

---

* supporter of the Prince of Wales   † supporter of the Prince of Wales
‡ carrying banner of the Red Dragon   § carrying banner of Llewellyn ap Gruffydd
¶ Secretary of State for Wales

leg – she spent her investiture day in Bangor hospital) and into the circular dungeon-like hall at the base of the Eagle Tower, where we shall be for the next sixty-five minutes until the Prince arrives.

There are a few small banners in this room, two loos in rooms that lead off, but otherwise bare stone and just the small entrance through which we have just come, and opposite, the steps up and out into the lower ward of the castle. Occasionally we can hear scraps of music and applause from the guests beyond but otherwise little sound from outside; the walls are so thick, that some of the succeeding processions appear to arrive almost silently, though I am told that they were all loudly applauded. There are about ten of these in all: the clergy, the Druids led by a figure straight from *The Arabian Nights*, with a lady at the rear carrying the Horn of Plenty, in which, so she later confided to Benjy, she had her sandwiches. Then came the Welsh members of Parliament, only about thirty strong as several such as Michael Foot had declined the invitation; they were a drab collection with hardly a morning coat between them, though Leo Abse brightened up the procession in a preposterous outfit.

Some members of these processions dropped off as they reached the Eagle Tower as they were to join either the Prince's or the Queen's procession, such as the Archdruid Cynan, an imposing one-hundred-per-cent Welsh figure who quickly collapsed into one of the few chairs available.

A procession of peers came, including Lord Beaumont of Whitley, which aroused much speculation among the bystanders – what possible Welsh connection can *he* have? Then a long and colourful line of mayors of Welsh boroughs, including the Lord Mayor of Cardiff, all in lace, kneebreeches and cocked hat, a vast improvement on his turnout for yesterday's rehearsal when he appeared in slacks and a shirt outside them, at which the Earl Marshal said, 'I hope you are not coming like that tomorrow.' Lots of maces, some borne by policemen, some by men who look like the doorman at the Savoy. The Yeomen of the Guard appeared, a fine colourful sight, including two ex-Welsh Guardsmen, Drill-Sergeant John MM and RSM Hedditch.

About this moment (2.15) we heard a 'boom', and Other Plymouth said to me, 'That's early for the twenty-one-gun salute,' and as it was not followed by others someone else said, 'Ha-ha, I expect it's a bomb.' Indeed it was, but fortunately on some waste ground a few hundred yards away, with no harm done and the two culprits were soon caught.

Now we have the Gentlemen-at-Arms arriving, perhaps the most elegant of all with their plumed hats and long axes. Some go forward into the castle accompanied by their colour, others join the rapidly swelling throng in this relatively small chamber. Next to arrive are the Peers and Gentlemen in the Queen's procession, the Earl Marshal, the Constable (dressed in his self-designed lift-boy type of outfit, *very* odd-looking and all in green, without a hat), the High Steward (Cobham), Henry Anglesey with the Sword of State, and a host of Heralds in their colourful tabards. Now the lesser royalties come in, Kents, Gloucesters (the Duke sadly absent), and Mountbatten. For the next ten minutes the room is like a high-powered cocktail party, many greetings and kisses being exchanged. I remain discreetly against the wall and talk to Morys Aberdare, magnificently gowned as Prior of the Order of St John of Jerusalem – he says there is a sort of under-garment which bothers him a bit. The Royals are finally formed up and sent on their way up the steps and into the castle ward – it makes me think a bit of what entering the Coliseum from a dungeon must have been like, the same cheering as you appear, but of course no lions.

All this time Snowdon chain-smoked (a particularly nauseating brand of Turkish cigarette, and strictly against the rules), much to Norfolk's obvious, though unspoken, displeasure, and the two appear to avoid each other as far as is possible in this confined space.

It is now time for us to form up in the centre of the chamber, and Ogmore and I leave a space in front of us for the Secretary of State to join in when he arrives with the Prince. A distant cheering gets louder and we hear the hooves of the Household Cavalry coming towards the gate; a flash of steel and plumes as they pass and then the carriage draws up. A quick glimpse of the Prince as he steps out, very smart dark blue uniform,* with the Garter sash, face a little

---

* He wore the No. 1 Blue (ceremonial) uniform of the Royal Regiment of Wales.

pale but confident, greeted by Snowdon at the top of the steps.

A breathless George Thomas comes in and takes his place. 'Your hair, George,' someone says and indeed he looks a little like Paderewski, so I hold his silk hat while he whips out a comb and tidies himself up. At last we are ready to move (the timing was miraculously on the minute, even after all these processions – the marshals had done a great job) and preceded by two Gentlemen-at-Arms we go slowly up the steps and, after an hour and five minutes, emerge like red-robed moles into the daylight. A sea of faces on either side, thunderous applause and a blood-tingling fanfare of trumpets from the ramparts high above our heads. The castle seems to stretch a long way and the Royal Dais, our final destination, looks a mile off. As the Prince appears in sight behind us the applause becomes terrific and then the band strikes up 'God Bless the Prince of Wales' and everyone joins in; this is a moment of great emotion and as we go slowly up the path I glance to the left to see an elderly guest with tears running down his face, still singing lustily. We reach the point in the 'waist' of the castle where the procession divides, those in front going on to their seats while we, led by the two banners, swing right to the Chamberlain Tower. The bearers of the banners halt and face about, one on either side of the very small door and in we go, up steps and down steps and into the quite small room where, on a table in the centre lies the Regalia. There is a note pinned to this table addressed to the Prince of Wales from Snowdon asking him to sign on the wooden top, which he duly does and adds the date. He looks a bit strained as he comes in but quickly relaxes and chats to various people; asks me if I am quite happy about the sword (it is very important that I hand it, with its belt, the right way to the Queen so that when she puts it over his right shoulder the hilt comes to the front on his left side – the secret is to have the buckle to the front as I carry it) and I reassure him.

There are two closed-circuit television sets placed in what was originally a huge open fireplace on one side of the room, and on these we can now watch the proceedings outside – at this moment the Queen's procession is approaching the Castle. Brigadier Goodchild (who is in charge of the Regalia) draws me on one side and says, 'I have just averted a nasty domestic crisis.' Apparently Princess Margaret had insisted that her two children should come down to this chamber to see the Prince and watch the television but the Earl Marshal said that on no account was the Prince to be bothered at this juncture. Goodchild took the only way out and asked the Prince if he would like to see them; fortunately he said yes, let them come, so they now appear with Nanny and are of course delighted with everything.

The Queen's procession has now arrived at the Water Gate and is received by a twenty-one-gun salute; the Constable presents the key of the castle, which she returns, and the procession starts on its way to the Royal Dais. Arrived there we have first 'Mae hen wlad yn hadau' and then 'God save the Queen'. We watch all this on the TV and it is a moving and intimate moment as our small party stand to attention in that little room with our Prince in our midst.

Garter is now despatched to summon HRH and on the set we watch him, oh so slowly, until he is right outside our front door. By now we have each got our piece of regalia in hand and though it is well nigh impossible to form up in that confined space we somehow get into the right order and shuffle out through the tiny medieval passage in single file, once more into daylight.

More fanfares, much longer this time, as we move towards the Royal Dais. Ogmore has a slight hitch with the coronet and I suddenly realise that he's no longer with me so mark time until he catches up. We go slowly up over the grass, the Prince makes his obeisance as he reaches the top of the steps, then goes forward to kneel on his stool in front of the Queen. Ogmore and I get to the top of the steps, bow and stay there.

Out of the corner of my eye I see the Earl Marshal in his place on my left and wonder if he is pleased with our performance so far – at least nobody has dropped anything and Heycock has not talked once since we left the tower.

The Home Secretary (Callaghan) reads the Letters Patent in English, very well too with plenty of emphasis at the right places. It is quite cool now, with a fair breeze so that one's robe blows about a bit occasionally and every so often one of the huge banners high up on the walls gives

The Investiture, 1969

a terrific crack like a whip as the wind lifts it up. The Queen looks serious, even severe, with Prince Philip on her left looking much more relaxed. She follows the reading from a text in her lap.

Now it is George Thomas's turn, in Welsh, and for the first time I begin to feel nervous; supposing my spurs get caught in my robe as I go up to the dais, have I get the buckle to the front, am I really meant to walk across the dais afterwards as Norfolk said – it looks so sacrosanct at the moment, where in heaven's name has he got to in the reading? Ah, here it comes, ' . . . af Fab Charles Philip Arthur George a'r Dywysogaeth honno a'r Iarllaeth honno, Trwy ai wrgegysu af a chleddyf,' and I am off, rolling no doubt, and get safely to the dais, halt, bow and hand the sword to the Queen, who takes it and puts it on the Prince. I walk half-left towards my seat behind the dais, where Benjy says, 'Very nicely done, Owen,' and I sit down and am much relieved to see the hilt of that *chleddyf* leaning forward, all proper thank God.

Ogmore has by now delivered the coronet (also tricky as there is a front and a back, unlike the 1911 one which appears to have been

183

round – interesting research could perhaps be done here on varying head-shapes of Princes of Wales throughout history), Maelor the ring, Haycock the Golden Rod, and finally Harlech the mantle, with which the supporting peers assist him and the Queen fastens the clasp. He is now invested with all the symbolic emblems of his Principality, and he next recites the Oath in a steady voice before the Queen exchanges the kiss of Fealty; he can now take a slight rest, sitting on his throne to the Queen's right, while Sir Ben Bowen Thomas reads the Loyal address. The Prince then replies, first in Welsh, then in English: what a musical voice he is blessed with! Long applause as he concludes, as much for his bearing as for what he has just said.

Ruth is sitting just to the right of the choir, in a wonderful position immediately behind Jeremy Thorpe, Heath, the Prime Minister and Mrs Wilson, the Lord Chancellor and others. Aunt Olwen, Valerie and Goronwy are away to the left, and the Aberconways I spy quite near. Immediately on my right is the orchestra and some twelve leading Welsh soloists, including Gwyneth Jones, Elizabeth Vaughan, Anne Howells, Geraint Evans, Ryland Davies, Trevor Anthony and others.

That is as far as my diary note goes, and certainly it covers my own personal involvement in the ceremony. Thereafter the Queen presented the Prince of Wales at three points in the castle, the last being at the King's Gate, and at each the royal family were received with enormous enthusiasm. The whole occasion went off so much better than anyone had expected and I believe its success can be attributed to two people in particular, Bernard Norfolk, who planned it meticulously and allowed nothing to be overlooked, and the Prince himself, whose bearing and clear dedication to his role in the Principality was manifest throughout. The day following the Investiture saw the start of his tour of Wales which went equally well, culminating in a very good party on board *Britannia* in Cardiff docks for all who had been involved in the ceremony. I talked on deck to Jim Callaghan who had not been on board before either: he said how pleased he was to be there, as his father had been an able seaman on the old *Victoria and Albert*, and how proud they were as children when he came home on leave in his smart uniform.

CHAPTER 17

An Abbey Occasion

In 1964 David went to Eton, to Peter Lawrence's house, and was followed there by Robbie a year later. Robbie then won a scholarship and went into College, where the master was Peter Pilkington, a first-rate teacher who later became headmaster of King's School, Canterbury, then St Paul's, and is now a life peer.

Anthony Chenevix-Trench was headmaster during this time, having previously been at Bradfield College where he had made a point of knowing every boy in the school by name, a practice which he endeavoured, unsuccessfully, to continue at Eton. One day he was walking along the High Street when a small boy failed to salute him; incensed, he hooked the boy with his umbrella and said, 'Don't you know who I am?' to which the boy said, 'No,' in a somewhat bored voice. 'I am your new headmaster,' said Chenevix-Trench. 'Oh Lord,' came the reply, 'then you must be some sort of relation.'

To his great credit Chenevix-Trench told this story against himself, claiming that it neatly summed up an Etonian attitude.

The lower-master at that time was Fred Coleridge, with whom David had various unhappy encounters; he was a friend of the Mounts and a frequent shooting companion at Wasing. David found himself frequently 'on the bill' and bottom of his division, so that after a couple of years it was agreed that it was time for a change and he went to Bradfield. This was quite a test of character for a boy of fifteen, having to leave his friends behind and start afresh, but he survived it with great fortitude and, two years later, spent a happy year with a French family near Clermont-Ferrand, followed by a spell in Hamburg with a shipping agency, thus becoming fluent in both French and German.

Robbie found himself in a particularly bright set of boys in College, including Philip Snow (son of the author), Martin Taylor and Tom Lyttelton. Competition was keen and they seemed to thrive in this hot-house of intellectual culture, though by the time they were sixteen or so, a spirit of rebelliousness against authority came to the surface, quite often when we were on holiday.

Julia, in the meantime, was a day-girl at Queen's Gate School before going on to the Sir John Cass Foundation (where she studied the history of art) and subsequently becoming apprenticed to a jeweller in Hatton Garden. She showed a real aptitude for jewellery design, and set up as a freelance designer – a career she has continued with great flair even after acquiring a husband and four children.

In 1970, a number of Liberal MPs and others pressed for a memorial to Taid to be placed in Westminster Abbey, twenty-five years after his death. Clough Williams-Ellis was asked to design the memorial, which was to be a simple slate slab, with the lettering picked out in colour; it was executed by Jonah Jones of Criccieth. I recall being in the Abbey one day when it occurred to me that the ideal position would be near to the stone slab commemorating Winston Churchill and in close proximity to the grave of the Unknown Soldier, which would thus link the two great war leaders. I was glad that the Dean and Chapter approved the suggestion. The Prince of Wales was to unveil the plaque and Jeremy Thorpe had agreed to give the address. Alas, three weeks before the event, Jeremy's wife Caroline was killed in a car crash; I told him that of course we would ask someone else but he insisted on going ahead, saying that it would give him something to concentrate his mind on: needless to say his address was perfect, and very moving.

I had been able to get the band of the Welsh Guards to play at the service, and with representatives from the Baptist Union of Wales, the Free Church Councils of Wales and the Governing Body of the Church in Wales all attending, the singing of the Welsh National Anthem (twice), plus 'Guide me, O thou Great Redeemer', I doubt if the Abbey had ever rejoiced in such a Welsh atmosphere before – it was all very exhilarating.

Part of the original plan had been that the Prime Minister, Harold Wilson, would hold a reception after the service at 10 Downing Street,

David, Robbie and Julia

but events had intervened and following the General Election in May Edward Heath was the new incumbent. He had barely had time to move in (his grand piano arrived that week) and so it fell to me to arrange a party.

I was very fortunate in being able to borrow, from the headmaster of Westminster School, Mr John Carleton, that beautiful building Ashburnham House, with its fine panelled room on the first floor. Uncle David was determined to meet the new Prime Minister so I introduced them, whereupon David thanked him for having fulfilled a pre-election gamble. Quite unmoved by this, Heath then told us that he had given a small party for all those who had been helping him during the campaign; a young man, the pilot of the aeroplane that had taken him all over the country, confessed that he had withdrawn all his savings to back Heath. 'I asked him what odds he had got for me,' said the PM, 'and he answered twenty-eight to one!' I enjoyed this self-deprecatory tale.

The only other occasion when I had any conversation with Mr Heath was a few years later, after he had ceased to be Prime Minister, in Pratt's where he was a guest of his doctor (Sir John Warren). It was the night that the bomb exploded across the road in Brooks's and Heath remained quite unperturbed.

I have explained in the previous chapter how I formed my own business in 1968; this developed rapidly, with the brokerage from the two McAlpine accounts forming a substantial proportion. Alfred McAlpine, my old employer, were to the forefront of motorway building and had, in 1958, built the very first stretch, the Preston bypass (now part of the M6). When the first seventy miles of the M1 was opened a year of so later, with no speed limit in force, I recall Jimmie McAlpine driving its entire length in a BMW in thirty-five minutes.

Being closely involved in the placing of all these insurances, I picked up the threads again with many of my old friends – with the result that in 1972 I was invited to join the board of Alfred McAlpine as a non-executive director, which gave me tremendous pleasure.

At about the same time I took on two other quite different activities. First, the Channel Tunnel Association asked me to become their

'Lloyd George knew their fathers', Savoy Hotel, 5 December 1973

A lunch for every prime minister or descendant thereof, this century:
Marquess of Salisbury; Lady Balfour (wife of present Earl of Balfour, great-nephew
of A. J. Balfour); Lady de la Warr (granddaughter of Campbell-Banneraman;
Paul Asquith (great grandson of H. H. Asquith); Lord Lloyd George; Lord Coleraine
(grandson of Bonar Law; Miles Huntington-Whiteley (Baldwin's grandson);
Malcolm McDonald (son of J. Ramsay McDonald); Mrs N. Chamberlain's niece
front row Winston Churchill (grandson); Lord Attlee (son); Lord Avon (Anthony Eden);
Harold McMillan; David Douglas-Home (son of Sir Alec);
Mrs Mary Wilson; Sir Edward Heath

president. This was a non-commercial, non-political group of enthusi-
asts whose sole object was to keep prodding government and private
enterprise to get on and build the tunnel. Our only asset, other than
the enthusiasm of the members, was a very extensive archive of
everything connected with the tunnel from its early beginnings in the
nineteenth century. Its president had always been a peer and I
succeeded a Labour life peer, Lord Popplewell, an engaging ex-trade
unionist and, appropriately, former engine driver; one of my functions
was to host an occasional reception in the House of Lords. We also
contrived to visit the early workings, and on one all-party outing we
went down the new pilot tunnel at Folkestone, then about a thousand

yards under the sea and as dry as a bone; across the channel, which we crossed by hovercraft, it was a different story, as at Sangatte, where the chalk band takes a sudden dip, they had serious water problems.

None the less, it was a great disappointment to all concerned when in 1975 the Labour government under Harold Wilson abandoned the project, on the grounds that the cost of the separate rail link to London, at £300m, was unacceptably high. It is ironic to contemplate that today (1999) this link has only just been started and will cost some £6,000 million. The muddled thinking that on the one hand allowed the tunnel itself to be built by private enterprise but on the other ignored the necessity for a high-speed rail link from London to Folkestone passes comprehension. But then the almost total blindness of successive governments in failing to invest in our railway system, while building immensely expensive motorways that have continually to be up-graded or widened, will emerge as one of the supreme follies of the twentieth century.

Having got that off my chest, I turn to the other and very different role that I took on in 1971 when I was appointed a member of the Historic Buildings Council for Wales, at the suggestion of my old friend, David Gibson-Watt, then Minister of State for Wales. This body, with its counterparts in England and Scotland, had come into being in 1953 following the Gower Report, and its main purpose was to advise the Secretary of State on the making of grants to listed properties. Some of these were well-known Grade I buildings, often in the care of the National Trust, such as Powys Castle, Chirk Castle or Erddig; but many were little-known gems of country houses hidden away up a lonely valley, and often in a shocking state of repair. Many owners were reluctant to apply for grant-aid, fearing that they would have to spend money they no longer had or that they would have to open their homes to public view. Our advisory architects and the other civil servants at the Welsh Office were ever sensitive to this sort of situation and had usually prepared the ground thoroughly before the council made a formal inspection; our then chairman, Major Herbert Lloyd-Johnes (known universally as 'Boy' and a descendant of Thomas Johnes of Hafod) had a wonderfully gentle way with these owners and if he suspected that their resources were more than they admitted to, had a fine knack of wheedling the truth out while at the same time persuading them that it was their duty to help us save their property.

Unfortunately a number of owners, out of pride or ignorance, left it far too late to ask for grant-aid, with the result that we sometimes arrived to inspect a house that was literally a death-trap; many of these have been well documented in Thomas Lloyd's *Lost Houses of Wales*.

We were a small body of seven members, including Henry Anglesey, who succeeded 'Boy' as chairman and who had given his family home, Plas Newydd, to the National Trust, Dr J. D. K. Lloyd, an antiquarian of great distinction, nine times mayor of Montgomery and known familiarly as 'The Widow', Professor Glanmor Williams, the Welsh historian, and Professor John Eynon, senior lecturer in architecture at Cardiff University. I was therefore very much the layman in such distinguished company but I immensely enjoyed my time serving on this council since it took me into corners of Wales I had never seen and created some lasting friendships. I retired in 1994, with much regret, but I was seventy and becoming increasingly deaf, which is a bore (for oneself and others) at meetings.

Following my mother's sudden death in 1966, Plas Gwyn was sold and David took up residence at the Oxford and Cambridge Club in Pall Mall where his South American parrot, 'Lorita', became a popular attraction in the bar. He later moved to the Reform, following his retirement from the Foreign Compensation Commission. At the time of my mother's death he was in hospital having an operation for a displaced retina; as a result of the shock he lost the eye. This gave him a somewhat piratical appearance, and with his habitual irascibility, he was not always an easy person to entertain, though when he held court at his favourite corner in the Reform he dispensed liberal measures of malt whisky with great generosity.

Goronwy was by now principal of the University College of Wales at Aberystwyth and gave me a graphic account of a visit that David once made there. Having met at the station at Shrewsbury, they headed west, stopping frequently for refreshment. David of course knew the area well from his days as the local county-court judge; in Montgomery he said they could not possibly pass through without seeing an old friend at the Dragon Hotel. In Newtown another old acquaintance would be horrified if he thought David had not stopped to pass the time of day and to take a glass for old time's sake; and in Llanidloes it was more than he dared to omit a call at the New Inn.

As the journey wound slowly on Goronwy became more and more alarmed; David was by now happily singing 'Calon Lân' and other old favourites from the great period of Welsh non-conformist revival. Finally they reached the hotel at Devil's Bridge; this was very popular with many of the lecturers (and students) from Aberystwyth and on this particular evening the bar was thronged. There was consternation when their highly respected principal entered supporting a very inebriated gentleman in full voice. When they eventually arrived at Plas Penglais and Valerie came out to greet him, he said huskily, 'Thank you so much for my visit.'

Poor David's emphysema became chronic and by the time of his eightieth birthday, which we celebrated with him in proper style at the Reform Club, he had moved into a retirement home at Putney and died there in 1986. In spite of the setbacks that had arisen towards the end of his career, he was widely mourned by his contemporaries in the legal profession, especially his fellow benchers at Grays Inn, and Valerie and I lost a devoted stepfather. Of the previous generation the only survivor was now Aunt Olwen, who continued hale and hearty, living with Benjy and Annwen at Criccieth, where she took great pleasure in collecting her pension weekly in cash at the post office, remarking occasionally, 'Well, my father did start it, after all.'

As someone once remarked, a divorce represents the end of a relationship and a public admission of failure; Ruth and I had not had an easy marriage for some time, the strains were only too apparent, but I know that I caused great pain when I left her in 1979; the hurt extended to my children, even though they were all in their twenties. My own parents having gone their separate ways when I was seven, I always vowed not to inflict the same misery on my own – but of course failed, and can only hope they have by now forgiven me.

CHAPTER 18

Return to the Land of My Fathers

Jo and I were married in June 1982 at Chelsea Registry Office, and thus began the happiest period of my life.

Josephine Gordon Cumming spent her childhood at Gordonstoun, that forbidding and haunted Keep in Morayshire where her family had dwelt for many centuries and which her father handed over to Kurt Hahn who started his school there in 1935. Thereafter her home was at nearby Altyre.

Her father died in 1939 while she was away at school and her mother, Betty, subsequently married Lord Cawdor, a near neighbour. Betty, a strikingly good-looking woman, was also a skilled and imaginative gardener and carried out wonderful improvements at Cawdor Castle. Jo's brother, William Gordon Cumming, had married Elizabeth Hinde, whose sister Cath became the wife of Hugh, the next Lord Cawdor, so there was much intermarriage between the two families.

Jo married first Roger Marquis (then Viscount Walberton), whose father was the redoubtable Fred, 1st Earl of Woolton, our wartime Food Minister and later chairman of the Conservative Party; I had met him a number of times (Uncle Gwilym was his number two at the Ministry of Food) and he was a regular at Edwin McAlpine's fabulous Christmas lunches at the Dorchester. At these occasions most of the cabinet seemed to be at the top table and we had rousing speeches from Harold Macmillan, Alec Home and Margaret Thatcher over the years. We would also be given a book, chosen by Edwin and generally written by one of his guests, though I do recall receiving *Dr Zhivago* one Christmas. These were great feasts which sadly came to an end when the family sold the hotel.

When Lord Woolton died in 1964 and Roger succeeded, he and Jo divided their time between Kenricks, a house near Henley which they rented from the Hambleden estate, and 31 Tite Street, which had been Sargent's studio and where the painter died in 1925. They had a son Simon, born in 1958, and a daughter Alexandra, born in 1961. To the great distress of all his friends, for he was much loved, Roger died very suddenly in 1969, at the age of forty-five.

Jo then married John, the 3rd Lord Forres, who was divorced from his wife Gillian. The Williamson family had extensive interests in South America through the family firm of Balfour Williamson, and John's grandfather had been a Scottish Liberal MP, the peerage being one of a number created by my own grandfather.

John, who had served in the Black Watch in the war and was ADC to our divisional commander in Italy, 'Naps' Murray, was an amiable soul but a hopeless alcoholic and Jo soon discovered what she had taken on: they were divorced in 1974 and John died four years later.

Our first home was in Bath, where I had bought the lower half of a house in Lansdown Crescent, looking over that delectable city, and with a small flock of Cotswold sheep (not ours) in the foreground. We then bought The Hall, at Freshford, six miles away. This was an elegant house built of Bath stone, somewhat in the Italian style, halfway down a steep hill that overlooked the River Frome. In both these places Jo displayed her considerable talent for home-making, as she has done later in Wales, of which more later.

In the early 1980s I was still working in London, dividing my time between Lloyd's and McAlpine's, who had a West End office. Life was very full and varied and I tried to keep an intermittent journal, from which I have taken the following extracts as examples:

Wednesday, 27 February 1985   I was a guest of honour at a Foyle's literary lunch for George Thomas (Viscount Tonypandy) to launch his somewhat contentious but very well-written and interesting book. He has been having treatment for cancer of the throat but, against doctor's orders, spoke for nearly twenty minutes, very vigorously. My neighbours at lunch were Harold Wilson – who was in the chair – and

Jo and the author

Manny Shinwell. Wilson is as much the egoist as ever: I mentioned Goronwy – 'Oh yes, I introduced him to his wife,' and I replied 'I know you did, she is my sister,' which he had forgotten (the great statistician's memory is slipping). His speech was as much a rehearsal of his own performance in Parliament as a tribute to George.

Shinwell, on the other hand, I found fascinating (he was one hundred years old last October). Feels that the only way ahead for Lords' reform lies in a revised committee system whereby Commons and Lords would be equally represented. Says talent in Lords is immense (how I agree) but it cannot *do* anything under present set-up. He says he has bad days – 'at my age one cannot expect to be 100% all the time', and sleeps little, waking often in the early hours and reading. Gets up at 7.30, shaves and washes, dresses himself and makes breakfast, later going to the Lords by taxi. Feels he is making a contribution there.

Spoke with admiration of LG but thought he was a 'rascal'

(morally). Went to Churt in 1940, at Churchill's request, to try to persuade LG to take on agriculture – nothing doing. Offered a drink, said he'd have whisky. LG said, 'You must have water with Irish whiskey, soda with Scotch.' 'And that,' Shinwell said, 'was all I came away with!' He was very fond of Gwilym, with whom of course he worked closely during the war.

I recall an earlier encounter with Harold Wilson, at Jesus College, Oxford, where I was Goronwy's guest. Geraint Evans, the great Welsh baritone, a fellow guest, was sitting opposite and asked, 'Harold, would you say you were musical?' to which Wilson replied, 'Not really. I think I was nearly six years old before I learnt that the Messiah didn't come from Huddersfield.

A somewhat different occasion appears in my diary.

19 February 1987 – Last week I went to Lord Stockton's memorial service in the Abbey. A great occasion, very crowded, with everyone one could think of there. Julian Faber read the first lesson, rather nervously but very well. Julian Amery the second, in his rich plummy voice. A superb address by Alec Home, absolutely right. The band of the Grenadiers played throughout, including the 'Grenadiers Return', a haunting piece I had never heard before, on pipes and drum, dying away to a whisper.

I heard a few days later (from Philip de Zulueta) that during the planning of the service the Dean had objected to the way in which the Grenadiers appeared to be taking over the musical side of things and pointed out that the Abbey had a perfectly adequate organ, etc. Alexander (Macmillan's grandson) said 'Oh well, Mr Dean, if you really feel like that I will have to appeal to higher authority.' The Dean, 'Who can you mean?' Alexander, 'I mean the Head of the Church of England and Colonel-in-Chief of the Grenadiers.' At which the Dean had to see the funny side of it and gave in, albeit with ill grace.'

I never knew Harold Macmillan well, only meeting him on a few occasions after he had retired from office, but I shall never forget the speech he made in Cardiff in July 1960, when he unveiled the statue of Taid by Michael Rizello in the Gorsedd Gardens.

I was sitting on the platform next to Philip de Zulueta, Macmillan's private secretary at the time, who suddenly whispered to me, 'He's thrown away his notes.' He had indeed, overcome by feelings of emotion and admiration for the man whom he had looked up to so much when he entered the Commons in 1924 and who had given him some gentle advice after his maiden speech. It was a most stirring tribute.

In July 1989 the French decided to mark the seventieth anniversary of the signing of the Peace Treaty at Versailles. The Anciens Combattants et des Victimes de Guerre invited the four grandsons of the signatories to attend the celebrations, putting us up in great comfort at the Trianon Palace Hotel. Our fellow guests were Pierre Clemenceau, aged eighty-seven, grandson of George Clemenceau, Vittorio Orlando, grandson of the Italian premier, and Professor Sear-Wilson, grandson of Woodrow Wilson; I was the youngest of the four by quite a margin, as indeed my grandfather had been seventy years before. The celebrations started with a very elaborate banquet in the Trianon Palace, with endless toasts and speeches, which mercifully did not require a contribution from me, since my French is execrable.

I had borrowed from Aunt Olwen the pen with which the treaty was actually signed and which had been for many years in the library at Brynawelon. Had I been called on to speak I had it in mind to flourish this article, saying, 'Voila la plume de ma tante!' – though, as Jo pointed out, the doubtful humour of this schoolboy joke would have been lost on our French hosts.

On the following day there was a most impressive parade, with contingents from each country dressed in 1918-style uniforms, tanks and other vehicles of the same date and an ancient motor car in which sat two actors impersonating Clemenceau and Poincaré. It was blazing hot sitting on the saluting base and we were thankful when the time came to be ushered into the Hôtel de Ville for refreshments and more speeches and to be presented with a medal apiece. It was altogether a very exhilarating day but one which clearly meant more to the French than the British, who virtually ignored the occasion.

During the 1980s, an appeal was launched to restore and enlarge the little museum at Llanystumdwy which housed my grandfather's freedoms and other memorabilia. At the same time, I handed over to Gwynedd County Council the next-door cottage 'Highgate' which, together with its adjoining workshop, had been Richard Lloyd's place of business and the house where David Lloyd George and his brother William spent their boyhood. LG's grave, on the banks of the Dwyfor, lies only a hundred yards away, so that within a very short compass visitors are able to see his childhood home, the museum celebrating his life and achievements, and his last resting place.

In December 1990 the museum was reopened by Lord Callaghan, who made an outstanding and compelling speech; Lord Cledwyn presided and I spoke on behalf of the family. During my remarks I played a tape of the old man addressing the 1935 National Eisteddfod at Caernarvon (in Welsh, of course) which was a huge success.

The Criccieth Festival came into being at about this time; as well as a varied programme of musical and dramatic events, there is an annual Lloyd George Memorial Lecture, at which, as patron, I have to introduce the speaker. Among the lecturers we have had Roy Jenkins and John Grigg, both outstanding historians, and in the case of the latter, Lloyd George's most distinguished biographer, whose fourth volume we all eagerly await.

Our visits to Criccieth for these and other occasions have always been made doubly joyful by the generous hospitality of Benjy and his dear wife Annwen, at the old homestead, Eisteddfa. Aunt Olwen remained there in her own part of the house, enjoying her grandchildren and keeping up all her local interests and old friendships, until she died shortly before her ninety-eighth birthday in March 1990. A lifelong Liberal and active in countless charitable causes (she was made DBE in 1969 for services to Wales), she was above all a devoted mother and grandmother; her death removed the last link between us and our grandparents.

I had first seen Ffynone* in 1971, when it was advertised for sale in *Country Life*, and was immediately taken by its beguiling atmosphere and

* pronounced Fur-nonny

Ffynone, Pembrokeshire

splendid position in that unspoilt corner of West Wales. But in those days I was up to my neck in the City, the M4 was only half built, and in any event someone else bought it quite quickly. Time went by, and thanks to an old friend, John Francis, who ran the leading estate agency in the area, I got to know the owner (who was only occasionally at the house), with whom I then had a protracted negotiation culminating in my buying it in 1987.

Since I had first seen the house it had suffered sorely from neglect: gutters had been left blocked, chimneys unswept, general decay unchecked everywhere, resulting in widespread dry-rot; the gardens were so overgrown that it was almost impossible to see where the paths led and fallen trees were entangled among the rampant brambles. Not surprisingly, Jo was somewhat downcast when I cheerfully announced that I had got the place, but she set about the restoration with great fortitude, engaging a friend in Bath, Enriqueta Crouch, a leading expert on the decoration of classical buildings, to help us.

Not many people immediately associate John Nash with Wales – he is more readily identified with the great terraces of Regent's Park or

Brighton Pavilion. But it was from South Wales that he came and, after an early disastrous building venture in London, it was to Carmarthenshire that he returned, bankrupt, in 1784. His mother set him on his feet again and, in 1792, he got his first commission, to build a gaol in Carmarthen. Other work followed and in the same year he received his first private order for the Vaughans at Golden Grove near Llandeilo. This was followed by his design for the octagonal library at that remarkable house Hafod, for Thomas Johnes, as a result of which he was taken up by the local gentry, including Colonel John Colby of Ffynone.

The Colbys had been settled in Wales for at least a hundred years, owning two other estates as well as Ffynone, namely Rhosygilwen and Pantyderi, and were among those masterful and sometimes eccentric families so well described in Herbert Vaughan's *The South Wales Squires*.

A medieval house was taken down and in 1793 Nash started work on a fresh site, high above the valley of the Dulas stream. The traveller and antiquarian Richard Fenton, writing in 1811, criticised its position, saying:

> then take a turn to the left, and, by a romantic winding ascent through most thriving young plantations up to the house of Fynonau [sic], a handsome modern building, the residence of John Colby Esq., but generally thought to be injudiciously placed on the summit of a very exposed hill, where the slope below it presented so many more eligible situations . . .

Any visitor today would surely agree that one of the glories of Ffynone is the stupendous view over the three counties of Pembrokeshire, Carmarthenshire and Cardiganshire.

Nash's design was very similar to that of other country houses he built in the neighbourhood, for example Llysnewydd (now destroyed) and Llanerchaeron, which he commenced a year after Ffynone and which is now owned by the National Trust. But it was at Ffynone that, encouraged by his patron, he allowed his imagination free range and, in the words of Nash's biographer, Terence Davis:

A shooting party at Ffynone

Ffynone was perhaps the most successful of Nash's early houses – quite plain, well-mannered and with a great sense of style. Inside, we see for the first time, in plan, detail and decoration, an original Nash interior; one which he was to use in the future in a variety of ways and on different scales.*

The house he designed stood four-square, with matching pediments on each elevation and the broad timber eaves forming deep tympana characteristic of Nash's work. Inside, all the principal rooms had elaborate plasterwork, and the staircase, of Painswick stone and in a cantilevered geometrical design, was a distinctive feature, elaborated on by Nash in much of his later work.

In the 1820s the entrance front was enlarged by a single-storey addition in the Greek Doric style; later in the nineteenth century the stable and service block was linked to the main house; finally, in 1904, a substantial remodelling was embarked upon. The Colby of the day

* Terence Davis, *John Nash: The Prince Regent's Architect*, Country Life, 1966

was a keen big-game hunter and before setting off on a year-long expedition to Siberia to shoot bears he told his wife, Annie, to carry on with the alterations as she pleased. On his return he was somewhat staggered at what he found, which included a substantial bill.

Francis Inigo Thomas, who carried out this work, was more of a garden architect than otherwise and had done great things at Athelhampton (in Dorset) and elsewhere, also collaborating with Sir Reginald Blomfield on *The Formal Garden in England* (1892).

As well as creating a new dining-room and adding a ballroom on to Ffynone, he fitted up the Nash dining-room as a library, and embellished the exterior of the house with rusticated stone quoins and heavy keystones above each window. Mercifully, he did not touch any of the exquisite Nash detailing of the interior. But it was outside that he exerted his true talents: on the west side, a formal square garden with yew hedging and semi-circular balustrading sprang up, while at the front of the house an elaborate belvedere was built out above a hundred-yard-long stone terrace, with grottoes at each end, one enclosing a water garden.

This then was the rather exotic structure that we took on in 1987 and upon which, over the next few years, exerted a lot of effort and spent a great deal of money. In this last respect we were greatly assisted by substantial grants from the Historic Buildings Council for Wales, to whose architects I shall always be grateful for their enthusiastic support and technical advice. Over the years we have had a steady stream of visitors from many different historical and antiquarian societies and I like to think that we have been able to give pleasure to these and other like-minded groups; Ffynone is now listed Grade I . The garden too has been rejuvenated; on our arrival it was hard to make out at all and I spent the first six months opening up half a mile of paths and creating new glades for replanting. Apart from the formal areas near the house that Inigo Thomas created, it is essentially a woodland garden, acid soil supporting a wide variety of rhododendrons and other shrubs, with a canopy of very well-grown, indeed superb, specimen trees.

If I have rhapsodised at too great length I can only plead guilty, but I have always longed for a home in Wales and Ffynone has filled so many

The Deputy Lieutenant and his wife

of the ideals that I sought – a classical house with a fine view, a tranquil situation and the possibility of an interesting garden. It is also large enough for relays of grandchildren to come throughout the seasons; I now have twelve and Jo has six, and with the sea only fifteen minutes away, we become very popular in the summer months.

I have also found myself drawn, very willingly, into a variety of local activities, in Pembrokeshire and further afield; currently the most exciting is the National Botanic Garden of Wales, where on a five-hundred-acre site the first botanic garden to be created in Britain for a hundred years is rapidly taking shape. I regard my retirement as being exceptionally enjoyable and in the words of the psalmist, 'The lines are fallen unto me in pleasant places; yea, I have a goodly heritage.'

Epilogue

I started to write this book five years ago and much has happened in the intervening period, including a steady increase in our family. David and Pam's two sons are both at Horris Hill, with William, the elder, due to go to Eton in September.

Robbie's investment-fund business, which he started in Hong Kong eight years ago, has grown rapidly and he has managed to survive the turmoil in the Far Eastern markets, as well as finding time to write two books. His eldest son (and my eldest grandson) Ricky is now sixteen and at Eton, and Alice is at Downe House; the younger children are at present with their mother Donna in Florida where she has just produced Robert Owen, my twelfth grandchild.

Julia and my son-in-law Simon Prior-Palmer divide their time between London and Appleshaw, his family home, with their four growing children.

William and Freddie with their Taid

*The author, Arthur, Nanny Stewart, George holding Harold,
Jo and Simon Prior-Palmer with Lara*

So, with Jo's six grandchildren making a total of eighteen, our life is a very full one and in the summer Ffynone sees a steady stream of visitors.

I have always been blessed with remarkably good health so it was something of a shock in my seventy fifth year to find that I had cancer. Two months of radio-therapy in that marvellous hospital, the Royal Marsden, seems to have done the trick for the time being and I have a great deal to be thankful for. I find gardening immensely therapeutic; to paraphrase a saying about farming, you should 'live as if you would die tomorrow and garden as if you would live for ever'.

Reviewing briefly the main strands of my working life since the age of seventeen, my old firm, Sir Alfred McAlpine & Son has, since Jimmie's death in 1991, sadly passed completely out of any family control. The founding firm of Sir Robert McAlpine & Sons Ltd, on the other hand, became a public company some thirty years ago, under the name of Newarthill (Grandad's birthplace). The family retrieved its private status recently and today, under the energetic leadership of my cousin Malcolm (H) and members of the fourth and fifth generation of the clan, the firm goes from strength to strength.

Alice, Robbie, Alexander, Donna, Ricky and Julia in Hong Kong

I have now been an underwriting member of Lloyd's for more than forty years and although, like many others, I lost a considerable sum of money during the late 1980s, I have just managed to hang on. With corporate capital now providing the lion's share of Lloyd's funds, the present ruling body seem determined to make it as difficult as they can for the traditional names, currently laying down a dubious rule whereby a substantial slice of earned profits is withheld on account of possible future losses. It remains to be seen for how long the loyalty of members can be tested in this way.

Finally, there is the House of Lords, well described as the best club in the world (barring White's of course), where I have enjoyed the privilege of membership for over thirty years. I cannot claim to have made a great mark there, it is not my bent, and I have no intention of putting my name forward for the lifeboat which it is intended will keep ninety-two hereditaries afloat pro tem. But I regret the manner in which its dismantlement is being carried out by a government whose motto might well be, 'Act now, think later.'

Enough. Suffice it to say I am content to gaze out on the lovely landscape of West Wales and to count my blessings.

Index